Bringing ABA
INTO YOUR INCLUSIVE CLASSROOM

Bringing ABA
INTO YOUR INCLUSIVE
CLASSROOM

*A Guide to Improving Outcomes
for Students with Autism Spectrum Disorders*

by

Debra Leach, Ed.D., BCBA
Winthrop University
Department of Curriculum and Instruction
Rock Hill, South Carolina

Baltimore • London • Sydney

Paul H. Brookes Publishing Co.
Post Office Box 10624
Baltimore, Maryland 21285-0624
USA

www.brookespublishing.com

Typeset by Aptara, Inc.®, Falls Church, Virginia.
Manufactured in the United States of America by
Sheridan Books, Inc., Chelsea, Michigan.

All examples in this book are composites. Any similarity to actual individuals or
circumstances is coincidental, and no implications should be inferred.

Library of Congress Cataloging-in-Publication Data

Leach, Debra
  Bringing ABA into your inclusive classroom : a guide to improving outcomes for students with autism spectrum
  disorders/by Debra Leach.
      p.   cm.
  Includes bibliographical references and index.
  ISBN-13: 978-1-59857-077-9
  ISBN-10: 1-59857-077-3
  1. Autistic children—Education.   2. Autistic youth—Education—United States.   3. Inclusive education—
  United States.   4. Developmentally disabled—Education.   I. Title.

  LC4718.L43 2010
  371.94—dc22

                                                                                                2010004177

British Library Cataloguing in Publication data are available from the British Library.

2014   2013   2012   2011   2010

10   9   8   7   6   5   4   3   2   1

Contents

About the Author

Debra Leach, Ed.D., BCBA, Assistant Professor of Special Education, Winthrop University, 701 Oakland Avenue, Rock Hill, South Carolina 29733

Debra Leach is a Board Certified Behavior Analyst. She previously served as a public school teacher, as an early intervention provider, and as the Associate Director for the Florida Atlantic University Center for Autism and Related Disabilities. Her main research interests include autism spectrum disorders, inclusion, applied behavior analysis, positive behavior supports, and early intervention. She enjoys training preservice teachers and working with school districts, families, and community groups to support the successful inclusion of children, adolescents, and adults with autism spectrum disorders across home, school, and community contexts.

Introduction

For decades now, applied behavior analysis (ABA) has been the intervention of choice for children with autism spectrum disorders (ASD) due to the fact that it is highly supported by research (Koegel, Koegel, Harrower, & Carter, 1999; Lovaas, 1987; McGee, Almeida, Sulzer-Azaroff, & Feldman, 1992; Pierce & Schreibman, 1995; Weiss, 2005). There are many different applications of ABA used with children with ASD, such as Discrete Trial Training, Pivotal Response Treatment, incidental teaching, and applied verbal behavior. All of these interventions are based on the original work of Baer, Wolf, and Risley (1968). These researchers published an article on the dimensions of ABA, presenting a framework for conducting single-subject research using behavior analytic principles to help make meaningful changes in the lives of individuals. These dimensions are now used as a framework for intensive intervention programs for students with ASD, not just for research purposes.

Although ABA has been shown to be effective, these teaching procedures are not often integrated into general education classrooms to support the inclusion of students with ASD. When students receive ABA intervention, it is often conducted in home settings, clinical settings, or in segregated classrooms in schools. This isolated type of service delivery does not often lead to generalization of learned skills across a variety of different settings and contexts (Lovaas, 1977; Spradlin & Seigel, 1982). It is quite difficult to provide meaningful learning opportunities using ABA for students with ASD when intervention is not implemented in natural settings, the places in which students will actually have to use the skills they are learning. Natural settings include everyday routines, activities, and places across home, school, and community contexts in which children participate regardless of whether or not they have a disability. At school, these settings can include playgrounds, cafeterias, hallways, and, of course, general education classrooms.

With recent federal mandates (Individuals with Disabilities Education Improvement Act [IDEA] of 2004 [PL 108-446]; No Child Left Behind Act of 2001 [PL 107-110]) supporting the inclusion of students with disabilities, more and more students with ASD are being included in general education classrooms. However, general education teachers often do not have the training and experience needed to meet the needs of these students. In 2001, the National Research Council, consisting of noted authorities in the field, made recommendations for what constitutes best practices for educating students with ASD. Among many recommendations, they suggested that children with ASD should receive specialized instruction in settings in which ongoing interactions occur with typically developing peers, interventions should be individualized

1

to meet their unique needs, they should be actively engaged in systematically planned instruction for at least 25 hours per week, and ongoing progress monitoring should be conducted. Thus general education classrooms would be the most appropriate settings for these recommendations to be addressed in schools to allow opportunities for students to engage with typically developing peers. However, simply placing students in general education classrooms does not address the other recommendations set forth. Even if the students are in general education classrooms for 25 hours per week, the amount of time in which they are actively engaged in activities aimed toward identified objectives is often much less than 25 hours. Using ABA interventions in general education classrooms ensures that instruction is individualized, systematically planned, and focused on addressing appropriate learning objectives and that progress is monitored on an ongoing basis. Parents will often request that their children with ASD receive ABA in the schools. Some school districts are complying with these requests by providing one-to-one ABA instruction in separate classrooms. This instruction is often implemented by paraprofessionals who do not have the required education, training, and experience to do so. Even if certified teachers implement these ABA interventions, the students often do not generalize the skills learned in isolated classrooms across a variety of natural contexts. Instead of fulfilling parent requests for ABA with a pull-out model, schools can develop ABA interventions that will be implemented in general education classrooms. Students will then be able to learn meaningful skills in the very contexts in which they are expected to use them. Not only will this address skill development, but also it will enhance their active participation in general education classrooms, which will increase natural learning opportunities as well.

Although implementing ABA in general education classrooms appears to be a clear way to address federal mandates and implement best teaching practices for students with ASD, there is little support for teachers to learn how to do so effectively. This book provides readers with the background information they need and procedures to follow for implementing ABA in general education classrooms. School-based teams can use this book to learn how to work collaboratively to assess the needs of students with ASD, set goals based on those assessments, plan ABA interventions to address the selected goals, and collect and analyze data to regularly monitor student progress. The appendix includes sample lesson plans in the areas of academics, behavior, social interaction, communication, and independent functioning. These plans can be used in their current form or altered to meet individual needs of students. The sample lessons include a multitude of examples for how ABA teaching plans can be developed, providing teachers with ideas as they design original plans for their students. A study guide is also included that teams can use to support its learning and facilitate the application of the material presented throughout the book.

1

Students with Autism in General Education Classrooms

This book discusses ways to successfully include students with autism spectrum disorders (ASD) in inclusive classrooms by using applied behavior analysis (ABA) teaching procedures to maximize learning. It is important to first have a clear understanding of the characteristics of students with ASD, the benefits and barriers of including students with ASD in general education classrooms, and best practices related to inclusive programming for students with ASD. By the conclusion of this chapter, you will also understand the rationale for using ABA teaching procedures in general education classrooms to best meet the needs of your students.

Overview of ASD

The term *ASD* is often used quite loosely. You may hear some people say that a student does not have autism, but is definitely "on the spectrum." If a student has some characteristics of students with autism, that does not mean one can say the student is on the spectrum. If a child is on the autism spectrum, it means that the child has autism, Asperger syndrome, or pervasive developmental disorder-not otherwise specified. These three disorders are the only ASD. They are under the larger category of pervasive developmental disorders, which also includes Rett syndrome and childhood disintegrative disorder, according to the *Diagnostic and Statistical Manual of Mental Disorders, Fourth Edition, Text Revision* (*DSM-IV-TR;* American Psychiatric Association [APA], 2000). For purposes of this book, characteristics of students with ASD are discussed without pinpointing the differences among these disorders.

Before discussing the impairments that students with ASD are likely to display, it is important to stress that students with ASD all possess unique strengths and talents.

Because ASD is a neurological disorder, their brains are not necessarily "wired" the same way as typically developing individuals. Thus students with ASD may in fact be able to do many things that most of their peers cannot do. Some students with ASD have amazing rote memorization skills that allow them to remember information that most people are unable to recall. Students with ASD may have talents related to art and music, enabling them to play instruments, sing, or create beautiful works of art. Other students with ASD may be gifted in certain academic areas or have such strong interests in certain topics that they know more about such topics than most people would ever know. It is important for teachers to first seek to find out what skills and talents students with ASD possess before focusing on all of the skills in which they have difficulty. By doing so, teachers can be sure to honor their students' special gifts and also access their strengths and interests as much as possible when teaching new skills or working on difficult tasks. Students with ASD, by clinical definition, have impairments in social interaction and communication and also have the presence of stereotypic behavior and/or a restricted range of interests (APA, 2000).

Impairments in Social Interaction

Students with ASD all have impairments in social interaction. However, not all students with autism will have the same type of difficulties. Some students may have impairments in the use of nonverbal behaviors such as eye contact, facial expressions, body posture, and social gestures. Students with ASD may not spontaneously seek opportunities to interact with other people. This does not necessarily mean that these students prefer to be alone, which is a descriptive characteristic that may be seen in a variety of informational materials related to autism. When students with ASD receive the supports they need to learn how to respond to the initiations of others, initiate interactions with others, and maintain interactions with others, they may indeed prefer these interactions over being alone. These skills related to interacting with others are referred to as *joint attention* and *social reciprocity skills,* core deficits in students with ASD (Jones & Carr, 2004; MacDonald et al., 2006; Mundy, 1995).

Joint attention entails two or more individuals sharing attention with one another related to a specific object, activity, or idea. Joint attention can consist of coordinating attention between people and objects, attending to a social partner, shifting gaze between people and objects, sharing affect and emotional states with another person, and being able to draw another person's attention to objects or events for the purpose of sharing experiences (Baldwin, 1995; Mundy, Sigman, & Kasari, 1990). This can be as simple as a student pointing to a bird in the tree on the playground, with the teacher responding, "Oh, wow! It's a blue jay!" Joint attention skills are also needed to engage in complex pretend play scenarios or instructional activities in the classroom. A basic way to understand joint attention is to think of it as the feeling you get when you feel like you are "in it together" when you are interacting with someone. When interacting with students on the spectrum, you may feel like you try really hard to interact and connect with a student, but you cannot get that connectedness that you get with other students.

Once a student with an ASD is connected with someone by establishing joint attention, the student then needs to use social reciprocity skills to engage in "the dance of human interaction," or long chains of back-and-forth interactions related to the object, activity, or idea in which they are sharing attention. Social reciprocity entails being aware of the emotional and interpersonal cues of others, appropriately interpreting those cues, responding appropriately to what is interpreted, and being motivated to engage in social interactions with others (Constantino et al., 2003).

Here is an example of social reciprocity being shared between a teacher, Mrs. Smith, and her student, named Rebecca:

Mrs. Smith: Good morning, Rebecca.

Rebecca: Good morning. I like your dress, Mrs. Smith.

Mrs. Smith: Thank you very much, Rebecca. Please turn in your homework. (*Rebecca turns in her homework.*)

In this example, Mrs. Smith and Rebecca shared two back-and-forth exchanges. Notice that the last exchange was not a verbal exchange. Rebecca simply complied with Mrs. Smith's request to turn in her homework. That is still a reciprocal exchange. When social reciprocity is being shared, exchanges can be verbal, or they can entail the use of facial expressions, gestures, or actions. Also, social reciprocity entails making initiations and responding to the initiations of others. In the example provided, Rebecca was able to respond to Mrs. Smith's greeting, and she also initiated an interaction by complimenting Mrs. Smith on her dress. Although social reciprocity skills develop naturally in typically developing children, students with ASD often require intensive interventions to learn how to engage in reciprocal social interactions.

Impairments in Communication

Students with ASD may have difficulty sending information and receiving information when interacting with communication partners. To engage in reciprocal social interactions, individuals need to use nonverbal and verbal receptive and expressive communication skills. Nonverbal communication can entail the use of eye contact, facial expressions, body posture, social gestures, and actions and the ability to interpret these nonverbal behaviors displayed by others. Communication skills can entail responding to or initiating interactions with others through the use of verbal responses, sign language, responding with the use of picture exchange, or the use of augmentative communication devices. Expressive language skills consist of the use of language to share knowledge, thoughts, and ideas with others. When students have impairments in expressive communication, they may have difficulty expressing their wants and needs, commenting, answering and asking questions, and engaging in conversations. When individuals with ASD do use expressive language, the words may be difficult to understand as a result of poor articulation. They may have trouble using appropriate volume, or they may display irregular prosody, which may result in sounding nasal or robotic. Receptive language skills consist of demonstrating understanding of language. When students have impairments in receptive communication, they may have difficulty responding to directions that require comprehension of language that is beyond their level of understanding.

Typically, people supplement verbal communication with nonverbal communication by using gestures, eye contact, facial expressions, and body posture to send messages to others. Many individuals with disabilities who lack verbal communication often use even more of these nonverbal communication skills to compensate for their lack of verbal skills, but students with ASD often do not do this. In fact, their lack of nonverbal communication skills often sends out the wrong message to their communication partners. For example, many students with ASD do not use appropriate eye contact when speaking with someone. That may send the message that they are not actually talking to someone in particular, when in fact they are. Also, if they do not use facial expressions to communicate their thoughts and feelings, they may be misinterpreted as being disengaged or disinterested, when that is not the case. When students engage with their peers, nonverbal communication such as eye contact, gestures, and facial expressions often help them connect with one another. Thus students with ASD often miss out on opportunities to establish connections with peers because of their limited nonverbal communication skills.

Some students with ASD may display stereotypic and repetitive use of language. This refers to a variety of idiosyncratic uses of language that an individual with ASD may display. This can include *echolalia,* or inappropriate repetition of something that was previously heard by the student (Stribling, Rae, & Dickerson, 2007). Echolalia is often considered a nonfunctional use of language; however, it is often used by a child with ASD as a means to communicate. For example, if a student is out of his or her seat in the classroom, the student with ASD may say, "I told you to stay seated," just like the teacher might have said at a previous time to another student. Although this verbalization may not be socially appropriate, it does serve a communicative purpose for the child. A child with ASD may also continually ask the same questions over and over again, such as, "When is your birthday?" or "How many pets do you have?" Again, this is not necessarily a nonfunctional behavior. Some students may engage in this type of behavior because they want to interact with others but do not have the skill set to do so appropriately. Thus they use echolalia to initiate interactions with others.

Other students with ASD may have *verbal self-stimulatory behaviors,* or *stims,* in which they verbalize certain sounds, words, phrases, or sentences in a nonfunctional manner. Often students who engage in verbal stims do so when they are not engaged in a meaningful interaction or activity. Therefore, it is important to get students actively engaged when they begin to use verbal stims as opposed to simply trying to stop the behavior from occurring.

Restricted Interests and Repetitive Behaviors

According to the *DSM-IV-TR* (APA, 2000), an individual with ASD will have at least one of the following characteristics:

- Marked preoccupation with one or more stereotypic and restricted patterns of interest that are abnormal either in focus or intensity

- Inflexible adherence to nonfunctional routines or rituals

- Stereotypic and repetitive motor movements

- Persistent preoccupation with objects or parts of objects

The first indicator refers to children with ASD who have a special interest in something that limits the capacity for a variety of interests. For example, a child may have a passion for trains and only want to play with trains and talk about trains. It is often recommended to utilize these special interests by using them to support students as they learn academic content, social skills, and positive behaviors and to enhance career development (Kluth & Schwarz, 2008).

Some individuals with ASD have a need for sameness in which they have a strong urge for certain things to be done a certain way each time. For example, a student may have a strong desire to follow the classroom routine exactly the same way every day. With even the slightest change in the class schedule, this student may engage in challenging behaviors. It is best to prepare students who have these needs for when a change is going to happen and to systematically teach them how to handle changes in routine in a positive manner.

Stereotypic and repetitive movements can include behaviors such as rocking, hand flapping, spinning objects, lining things up, or any other movement without a functional purpose that the student displays often. Some students with ASD have an interest in parts of objects, such as wheels on a toy car. Thus, when they pick up a toy car, they don't necessarily play with it as other students may play, but instead they focus on spinning and examining the wheels and how they work. These types of stereotypic behaviors usually occur when a student is disengaged from meaningful activities, just as was discussed with verbal self-stimulatory behaviors. Thus it is crucial to positively redirect students back to engaging activities when these behaviors arise, as opposed to simply trying to get the students to stop doing them.

Benefits of Including Students with ASD in General Education Classrooms

There are many benefits of including students with ASD and other disabilities in general education classrooms. Some parents and educators think in terms of the idea of "social inclusion." This idea makes the assumption that students with ASD are being included almost solely to benefit from the social experience. Being included in general education classrooms is certainly vital when it comes to developing social interaction skills with peers. Therefore, including students to provide them with opportunities to develop such skills is obviously positive. However, inclusion also benefits the students by providing more opportunities for accessing the general education curriculum than they would have otherwise, for developing communication skills within the context of a natural setting such as the general education classroom, for increasing their use of positive behaviors, and for learning how to learn alongside their typically developing peers to prepare for life beyond public school settings. The opportunities that general education classrooms provide for developing social skills, communication skills, academic skills, positive behaviors, and coping skills cannot simply be replicated in a special education setting (Chandler-Olcott & Kluth, 2009; Diehl, Ford, & Federico, 2005).

Barriers to Including Students with ASD in General Education Classrooms

Frequently it is the belief systems of others that prevent inclusion for students with disabilities. For example, many special educators truly believe that children with ASD need to be taught in self-contained classrooms in order to benefit from instruction. Many general education teachers do not feel that they are able to meet the needs of students with ASD in their classrooms. Many parents of students with ASD think their children need specialized settings to reach their full potential. Many parents of typically developing students do not want their children to lose out because they have a child with a disability in their classroom. The fact of the matter is that self-contained special education settings are not "curing centers." There are no magic tricks to cure children with disabilities in these settings. Yes, intensive one-to-one instruction may be provided in self-contained settings, which may be quite helpful. However, what about all the other learning opportunities beyond one-to-one instruction with a teacher? Where is the peer interaction to promote social skills and communication skills development? Where is the dynamic of the academic interactions among the students in a general education classroom that provides great learning opportunities across a variety of domains for all children? Although general education teachers often do not have the training and experience in working with students with ASD that is required to successfully include these students in their classrooms, it is the job of special educators to transfer their knowledge and expertise to the general education teachers. This can be done through training, modeling, coaching, and collaboration to allow general education teachers to enhance their skills so they can meet the needs of all their students. Most of the teaching strategies that are helpful for students on the autism spectrum are also useful for typically developing students. When general education teachers and special education teachers collaborate, both parties are able to learn from one another to become the best teachers they can for all students. For decades, research has clearly shown that students with disabilities and students without disabilities benefit from inclusive classrooms that follow the recommendations of best practices for inclusive education (King-Sears, 2008; Odom, Deklyen, & Jenkins, 1984; Staub & Peck, 1994).

Best Practices for Including Students with ASD in General Education Classrooms

For students with ASD to have success in inclusive classrooms, general education and special education teachers must work together to create positive learning environments, appropriate and engaging instructional activities, and a system of supports within the classroom that allows all students to learn. To create such classrooms, educators should use positive behavior supports (PBS), differentiate instruction, utilize teaching strategies that promote active engagement, and appropriately utilize the professionals and paraprofessionals in the classroom.

Positive Behavior Supports

PBS or positive behavioral interventions and supports (PBIS) are based on a three-tier system of schoolwide behavior support (Bradshaw, Reinke, Brown, Bevans, & Leaf, 2008):

Tier 1: Schoolwide and/or classroomwide behavioral expectations with consistent positive consequences

Tier 2: Behavioral interventions for specific groups of children requiring additional supports

Tier 3: Individual behavioral interventions for students needing intensive levels of support

PBS is a proactive approach rather than a reactive approach. Instead of responding to inappropriate behavior after it occurs and providing punitive measures, specific behavioral expectations are systematically taught and consistently reinforced in a positive way. Students with ASD who are included in general education classrooms will benefit when the classroom rules and procedures are explicitly taught and when they receive contingent reinforcement when meeting the expectations and positive redirection when they are not. Students with ASD may need interventions at Tier 2 and Tier 3 to be able to learn the positive behaviors needed to be successful in the general education classroom. Often Tier 3 consists of conducting functional behavioral assessments to determine the function(s) of a student's challenging behaviors in order to develop a behavioral intervention plan. Behavioral intervention plans may include changes to the environment, changes to teacher and/or peer behavior, and goals for the student that may serve as replacement behaviors or new skills. To increase the success of students toward achieving their goals in behavioral intervention plans, ABA procedures can be used. The chapters that follow provide information and procedures related to implementing ABA teaching in the general education classroom to promote the learning of positive behaviors, communication skills, social interaction skills, academic skills, and independent functioning skills.

Differentiating Instruction

Differentiated instruction is an approach to teaching a diverse group of students that meets the unique needs of each learner within the group. The rationale for differentiating instruction is that all students benefit from a variety of instructional methods and supports (Lawrence-Brown, 2004). Carol Ann Tomlinson (1999) discussed how classroom instruction can be differentiated across content (what the students learn), process (how the students learn), and product (how the students demonstrate mastery) to address the students' readiness levels (what is developmentally appropriate for individual students), interests, and learning profiles (how students learn best). This type of instruction is essential for students with ASD to be successful in inclusive classrooms. Teachers need to set learning goals that are developmentally appropriate for these students, provide access to the material through a variety of modalities, and allow students to demonstrate what they have learned in a variety of ways.

Increasing Active Engagement

To keep students with ASD actively engaged in instructional activities, teachers need to use a variety of strategies. If a student is engaging in self-stimulatory behaviors or other stereotypic behaviors, it may be because the student is not engaged in the lesson. Therefore, teachers should then focus on what they can do to enhance their instruction to reach that student instead of focusing on how to stop the undesirable behavior. Some ways to keep students with ASD actively engaged during instruction are included in Table 1.1.

Appropriate Use of Professionals and Paraprofessionals

The way in which professionals and paraprofessionals are utilized can make a world of a difference when it comes to including students with ASD in general education classrooms. Special education teachers often view their role as coming into the classroom to work directly with a child. This often translates into the special education teacher pulling up a chair next to the student or hovering over the student while providing help during ongoing instructional activity. Although this may be useful in some situations, the main role of the special education teacher is to provide the necessary supports to the general education teacher so that teacher can meet the needs of that student throughout the school day. This may include co-teaching lessons to model effective strategies, observing and providing feedback to the general education teacher, meeting with the general education teacher to discuss areas of need and problem solve together, helping to generate data collection procedures that are easy to implement in the general education classroom, and generally becoming a coach for the general education teacher as the teacher learns how to effectively include the student

Table 1.1. Ways to keep students with ASD actively engaged in lessons

Make sure learning objectives are developmentally appropriate.
Use concrete examples to help students connect new content with their existing knowledge.
Circulate within the classroom and give feedback/reinforcement.
Ask a lot of questions.
Have students work collaboratively to solve problems and complete tasks.
Ensure success by using prompting/fading procedures and behavioral momentum (see Chapter 5).
Maintain a brisk pace of instruction.
Illustrate content with stories.
Use guided notes.
Use choral responding.
Connect content to everyday life.
Give clear and concise directions and ensure understanding.
Access students' strengths and interests as often as possible.
Give students choices.
Use activities that arouse curiosity.
Use advance organizers.
Vary grouping arrangements.
Utilize multimedia when presenting information.
Incorporate music and art into instructional activities.
Encourage brainstorming.
Use manipulatives and other hands-on activities.
Role-play.
Have students use gestures during lessons.
Use games.
Have students create/do something during instruction.
Have students come up to the board.
Utilize technologies such as computers, Promethium boards, and smart boards.
Assign partners and have students share responses to questions with their partner.
Be enthusiastic and encouraging.
Remind students of behavioral expectations often.
Be much more positive than negative/corrective.

with ASD in the classroom (Murawski & Hughes, 2009). It goes without saying, however, that the best scenario is one in which the general education teacher and special education teacher are co-teaching all day long. However, this is often not the case as a result of budgetary constraints and the way schools are organized.

Paraprofessionals (teacher assistants) must not be used as "shadows" or one-to-one assistants for students with ASD in general education classrooms. Although it is true that students with ASD may require some one-to-one instruction and consistent redirection and reinforcement, that does not mean that one individual should be "glued" to the student. When a student in a classroom requires a great deal of support, a paraprofessional can be assigned to the classroom to enable the teacher(s) to better meet the needs of all students. A paraprofessional can provide some one-to-one support to the student with ASD, but that person can also assist with the other students in the classroom to enable the teacher to provide the necessary supports to the student. It may be that during independent work time, the paraprofessional is circulating and supporting the majority of the class while the teacher is providing one-to-one instruction to the student with ASD. There are many negative consequences that may arise when a paraprofessional is assigned to one specific student (Broer, Doyle, & Giangreco, 2005). Some examples are as follows:

- The student is isolated socially from peers.

- The paraprofessional's supports are distracting to the student and other students in the classroom.

- The teacher gives up much of the teaching responsibility to the paraprofessional.

- The student becomes dependent on the paraprofessional to complete work.

To prevent these things from happening, it is important to utilize the paraprofessional more as a second teacher in the classroom working under the guidance of the general education teacher.

Chapter Summary

Although utilizing the best practices discussed in this chapter will certainly promote the successful inclusion of students with ASD, most students on the autism spectrum will require additional supports to learn some academic skills, social skills, communication skills, independent functioning skills, and positive behaviors. These additional supports must be provided to ensure students are receiving a free and appropriate public education as required under special education law. It is true that students with ASD will learn many skills and concepts when actively engaged in an inclusive classroom. However, when these students are having difficulty learning specific skills and concepts, the use of more explicit teaching procedures may be necessary. Teaching procedures that utilize principles of ABA have been shown to be effective for teaching students with ASD a variety of skills (Weiss, 2005). A common misconception, however, is that ABA can only be implemented by individuals with specialized training in ABA, and it must be done in one-to-one settings. As you will learn in Chapter 2, the definition and description of ABA does not say as such. In fact, to increase motivation and promote generalization, it is often recommended that ABA teaching procedures are implemented in natural settings across home, school, and community environments. The general education classroom is the most natural setting in the school environment. The remaining chapters provide an understanding of ABA and provide guidelines for using ABA teaching procedures in inclusive classrooms.

2

Understanding ABA

• •

This chapter provides a brief history of the field of ABA by beginning with an overview of behaviorism and how it served as the basis for ABA. A description of the seven dimensions of ABA are provided, along with explanations for how these dimensions can be met when implementing ABA interventions in general education classrooms. Specific applications of ABA for working with students with ASD are discussed, including Discrete Trial Training (DTT), Pivotal Response Training (PRT), incidental teaching (IT), and applied verbal behavior (AVB). The chapter concludes with a summary for how ABA can be implemented in general education classrooms.

History of Behaviorism

ABA is based on principles of behaviorism, which is a theory of learning based on the idea that all behaviors are learned through conditioning. There are two forms of conditioning: classical conditioning and operant conditioning. *Classical conditioning* entails pairing a neutral stimulus with a naturally occurring stimulus to get the same response for the neutral stimulus that is evoked from the natural stimulus. In the early 1900s, Ivan Pavlov experimented with classical conditioning in his studies with dogs. The natural stimulus was food, and the response was salivation. The dogs would salivate when presented with food. Pavlov was able to show that you can teach the same response with a different stimulus by pairing. Each time the dogs were presented with food, a bell would ring. Each time the dogs would salivate. Eventually, when the bell rang even without the presence of food, the dogs still salivated. Thus the dogs were conditioned to salivate when they heard a bell ring.

Operant conditioning is based on the work of B.F. Skinner and is a method of learning through the use of rewards and punishment. From the 1930s to the 1950s, Skinner conducted many studies to show the effects of consequences in the environment on behaviors. One of his most famous studies entailed teaching pigeons to peck on a lever to obtain food using positive reinforcement. Each time the pigeons pecked on the lever, a pellet of food was dispensed. Thus the pigeons learned to increase their behavior of pecking on the lever to get food. Procedures such as positive reinforcement, negative reinforcement, punishment, extinction, and shaping are all principles of operant conditioning that are used today as part of ABA intervention programs.

History of ABA

In 1968, Baer, Wolf, and Risley published their landmark article "Some Current Dimensions of Applied Behavior Analysis" in the first volume of the *Journal of Applied Behavior Analysis*. In this article, they presented a framework for conducting applied behavior analytic research. This framework consisted of seven dimensions that must be present for single-subject research to be considered ABA. Today, this framework is also used for implementing ABA intervention programs that are not necessarily designed for research purposes. Whether using ABA for research or daily intervention programs, it is still defined by the seven dimensions. These dimensions consist of the following:

1. Applied

2. Behavioral

3. Analytic

4. Conceptual

5. Technological

6. Effective

7. Generality

Each of these dimensions is discussed in detail next and is summarized in Table 2.1.

Table 2.1. Dimensions of ABA

Dimension	Explanation
Applied	The intervention is designed to have a meaningful, positive impact on the life of the individual.
Behavioral	The goal can be directly observed and measured. The objective is defined so clearly that the behavior can be measured by different people in the same way.
Analytic	Data show that the intervention is responsible for the change in behavior.
Conceptual	Strategies and interventions used utilize researched principles of behaviorism.
Technological	The teaching procedures are written so explicitly that different individuals can implement them in exactly the same manner.
Effective	The intervention results in significant positive changes in behavior.
Generality	The skills learned can be maintained over time and utilized across different settings and contexts.

Source: Baer, Wolf, and Risley (1968).

Applied

An intervention is *applied* if it has immediate face validity (Baer et al., 1968; Baer, Wolf, & Risley, 1987; Bailey & Burch, 2002). In other words, applied means that the intervention is implemented to make meaningful changes in the life of an individual. This expectation is met by setting appropriate goals for the ABA interventions (see Chapter 4). The requirement from special education law (Individuals with Disabilities Education Improvement Act [IDEA] of 2004 [PL 108-446]) that individualized education program (IEP) goals be functional goes hand in hand with the requirement that ABA interventions be applied. If a goal is functional, it is meaningful for the student and will enhance the student's participation in the academic curriculum and/ or enhance the student's quality of life.

Some goals that are set for students with ASD are not always meaningful for a student. For example, one-to-one ABA programs may include goals such as imitating block designs, matching two-dimensional objects to three-dimensional objects, or matching an object to the appropriate category. These types of goals may not necessarily have meaning to the student across a variety of natural contexts or enhance the quality of life for the student. Instead, goals can be set to enhance the communication and social interaction core deficits of students with ASD, such as imitating peers in play, pointing to pictures of desired items to make requests, or describing an experience using a complete sentence. When goals such as these are mastered, they are useful across a variety of settings and enhance the social and academic experiences of students.

Behavioral

Behavioral means that the goal set for the ABA intervention is observable and measurable. If the goal is behavioral, the focus is on what the student actually does as observed and recorded by another person (Baer et al., 1968, 1987; Bailey & Burch, 2002). A nonexample of an observable goal would be one stating that the student will be happy. Happiness is not necessarily something that can be seen. Although some people may clearly show happiness by smiling or laughing, the happiness of others may not be as easy to actually see. Instead, a goal can be observable by stating that the student will make eye contact with a peer when the peer joins the student in play. If the goal is measurable, it means that different people collect data on student performance in the same way. This is achieved by clearly defining the behavioral expectation. For example, if the goal states that the student will remain on task during independent work time, keep in mind that different adults may measure that differently. On task can mean writing, talking, reading, raising a hand to answer a question or ask for help, drawing, or a variety of other behaviors. Thus, when writing a goal, it is important to clearly define the behaviors that will be required to fulfill the expectation.

Analytic

Analytic means that there is a functional relationship between the procedures implemented and the actual behavior change (Baer et al., 1968, 1987; Bailey & Burch, 2002).

In other words, the interventions being implemented with the student are responsible for the changes in behavior. In a research design, this can be shown in a variety of ways, such as through multiple-baseline designs, reversal designs, and repeated measures. With these research methods, data are collected systematically to be able to show that the intervention is responsible for the changes in behavior. However, when implementing ABA interventions in general education classrooms that are not used for research purposes, it is somewhat difficult to fulfill this dimension of ABA. Typically, teaching designs are used when implementing daily behavioral interventions. Teaching designs consist of taking baseline data and intervention data only. Realistically, this is usually as far as teachers are able to go to document that the intervention is responsible for the change in behavior.

So, to meet the analytic dimension of ABA teaching, it is important for teachers to at least collect baseline data before beginning any ABA intervention. Teachers often do not collect baseline data when implementing different teaching strategies and thus have a difficult time knowing whether the intervention is resulting in significant change. For example, if a student is displaying calling-out behaviors during classroom instruction, teachers may try a variety of different strategies to reduce such behaviors and increase hand raising. However, teachers often do not take baseline data on the number of call-outs before implementing a new strategy. This is what is required when implementing ABA interventions.

Baseline data must be collected before the intervention begins to obtain information on the behavior being targeted before intervention. Then, data must be collected while the intervention period is in place to determine whether the behavior is changing due to the methods being used. This is very important because teachers often stop implementing interventions that are actually working because they think they are not working. In the previous example, if the student was still calling out even after the interventions were in place, the teacher may decide to stop the intervention. However, data may show that the frequency of call-outs is decreasing from the baseline level, and the teacher would then be encouraged to continue the intervention. If baseline data are taken and graphed, teachers can visually see that the interventions are working.

Conceptual

Conceptual means that the teaching procedures being used as part of an intervention are based on principles of behaviorism (Baer et al., 1968, 1987; Bailey & Burch, 2002). This may entail the use of reinforcement procedures, prompting/fading procedures, shaping, time delay, behavioral momentum, task analysis, direct instruction, self-monitoring, extinction, and so forth, to name just a few. Chapter 5 provides detailed descriptions for these strategies and others, including definitions and examples.

This dimension of ABA simply requires that the teaching procedures being used incorporate strategies that have been shown to be effective through behavioral research.

A teaching procedure may be quite effective, but if it does not include the use of behavioral teaching strategies, it cannot be considered ABA. For example, if a student learns to line up appropriately by watching other students without the use of any other behavioral interventions, that is an effective teaching procedure, but it does not meet the conceptual dimension of ABA. However, if watching other students is not enough for the student to learn to line up, and the teacher must use prompting/fading procedures to teach the student to line up, then the conceptual dimension of ABA has been fulfilled.

Technological

The *technological* dimension has nothing to do with what most people think of when they hear the word *technology*. It means that the teaching procedures are written in such a clear, explicit manner that any person implementing the procedures would conduct the exact same methods (Baer et al., 1968, 1987; Bailey & Burch, 2002). The key word here is *written*. It is very difficult to meet the technological requirement without writing the teaching procedures down. Although it is true that a group of individuals implementing an ABA intervention can meet to discuss how the teaching will be conducted, it is rare that these discussions alone would result in each person implementing the intervention in exactly the same way. Thus writing the procedures down for all to refer to is best.

Chapter 7 provides examples of ABA lesson plans that are written to meet the technological dimension, and Appendixes A–E provide additional sample lesson plans. It can be time-consuming to write teaching procedures when you begin implementing ABA interventions. Therefore, these samples provide a bank of teaching procedures you can use with your students to reduce the time spent on developing teaching procedures. Of course, you will likely have to make some modifications to the teaching procedures to meet the individual needs of your students, and you will likely have goals you want to address that are not included in the samples. However, you will find that once you experience writing the procedures, it gets easier and easier to develop teaching procedures that are conceptual the more you practice doing so.

Effective

Effective means that the intervention being used is making meaningful and significant changes for the student (Baer et al., 1968, 1987; Bailey & Burch, 2002). How do we determine what is considered significant change? Baer et al. (1968) suggested asking yourself the following question: How much did the specific behavior need to be changed? For example, if you were implementing an intervention to improve positive social interactions with peers and reduce aggressive behaviors toward peers, the aggression would need to diminish greatly for the intervention to be considered effective. If a student hits other students 20 times per week during baseline and only reduces to 15 times per week after interventions are implemented, then that is not enough behavior change to be considered effective. The student would need to drastically reduce aggression toward peers for the intervention to be considered effective. If the student reduces to 5 or fewer aggressive acts toward peers each week from 20, it is probably safe to say that the intervention is effective.

The effective dimension is actually where the data analysis comes into play. Teachers often take data when implementing ABA interventions. However, simply taking data is not enough. Teachers must analyze the data to make instructional decisions. The best way to do this is to always have a graphical display of the data you are collecting. You cannot analyze your data by having pages and pages of data sheets that you collect in a binder of some sort. For each goal, you should have a graphical display of the student's progress. Then you must examine the data to determine whether the student is making adequate progress or not. Chapter 5 provides a variety of ways to collect and graph data, and Chapter 6 provides methods for interpreting data for making instructional decisions.

In research designs, effective also pertains to reliability. This means that the interventions being used have been shown to have positive effects with a variety of individuals across a variety of different contexts and situations. Simply put, an intervention is reliable when it is implemented repeatedly with different individuals and the results are positive for all or most of the individuals receiving the intervention. This goes hand in hand with the conceptual dimension. Research has shown the reliability of interventions designed for students with ASD that utilize principles of behaviorism such as positive reinforcement, shaping, prompting/fading procedures, behavioral momentum, and time delay (Davis, Brady, Hamilton, McEvoy, & Williams, 1994; Lovaas, 1987; McGee, Almeida, Sulzer-Azaroff, & Feldman, 1992; Pierce & Schreibman, 1995). Thus ABA interventions utilize these strategies because of their consistent reliability, and that is why they are part of the conceptual framework of ABA teaching procedures.

Generality

Generality means that the skills the student learns are used across a variety of contexts and situations. The ability of students with ASD to generalize what they learn is often documented as a difficulty (Gresham & MacMillan, 1998). Therefore, educators must carefully plan for teaching students to generalize the skills they are learning as opposed to just hoping they will do so. If ABA intervention programs meet the applied dimension and develop goals that are meaningful for the student across a variety of contexts, it is much easier to plan for generalization. For example, if the goal consists of teaching a student to greet others, then the teaching procedures can be implemented in the general education classroom, in special area classrooms, in the cafeteria, in the hallway, and on the school bus. Another way to plan for generalization is to do what Stokes and Baer (1977) called "training loosely." This means that you vary the way you present requests to your students so they learn how to respond no matter how a request is made. This also means accepting a variety of different appropriate responses from the student as opposed to teaching only one specific response.

The following scenario clearly explains the importance of training loosely when working with students with ASD:

> Brian, a 5-year-old boy with autism, was learning how to respond to greetings. The intervention being used was very specific. The adult would say, "Hi, Brian!" and Brian would then have to say, "Hi," followed by the adult's name. Well, one day Brian was at the community park with his mother. A stranger wearing a yellow shirt said, "Hello!" to Brian. While it was great that Brian knew to respond even though the woman said "hello" and not "hi," it wasn't so great that he said, "Hi . . . yellow" because he didn't know the woman's name. He knew the right answer meant "hi" and then the name, so he came up with the closest thing he could think of. This was definitely quite humorous, but clearly a perfect example for why there shouldn't be such specific expectations for responses. Instead, Brian should have learned that he could say "hi" and the person's name or just "hi" or "hello" or "hey" or any other appropriate greeting.

Applications of ABA for Students with ASD

In the late 1970s, researchers began applying ABA to students with ASD. A variety of specific applications of ABA have been developed since then to help students with ASD learn. The following section provides an overview of a few of these applications of ABA for students with ASD, including DTT, PRT, IT, and AVB. These are the most common ABA procedures used when working with students with ASD, and it is important for teachers to understand these valuable teaching methods in order to learn how to utilize them in appropriate ways in the general education classroom.

Discrete Trial Training

DTT is an ABA teaching procedure that entails breaking skills down into discrete tasks and using a structured behavioral teaching approach to ensure mastery of each skill (Lovaas, 1987). DTT uses an A-B-C teaching format. The A, or *antecedent,* represents an opportunity for the student to respond to a specific stimulus. The antecedent may be a question, a direction, a comment, a gesture, or any other stimulus that would require a response. The B, or *behavior,* is an appropriate response to the antecedent that the student displays. The C, or *consequence,* is positive reinforcement that is delivered after the appropriate behavior.

Of course, if the student does not have the skill that is being taught, it is not likely that the student will be able to respond to the antecedent without some assistance. This assistance would be in the form of a prompt. A *prompt* is a cue that can be verbal, gestural, or physical. It is given after the antecedent to enable the student to successfully display the desired behavior. Then positive reinforcement is given. Eventually the prompts are faded out until the student can respond without any prompts at all.

With DTT, multiple learning opportunities, or *trials,* are presented to the student to promote learning mastery. These trials may be presented multiple times in a row. This is called *mass trialing.* However, multiple trials can be implemented throughout the student's day as well. The most important thing about DTT is that it prevents empty requests being made to students with ASD. Often teachers will present an antecedent (question, comment, direction), but a student will not respond. This would be an empty request if the teacher then calls on a different student or moves on to something else. Instead, with DTT, the teacher would deliver a prompt to enable the student to respond successfully and then use positive reinforcement after the response.

Embedded discrete trials is a strategy that will be discussed in Chapter 5. This strategy uses the A-B-C teaching sequence embedded within ongoing classroom routines and activities. Other behavioral strategies used when implementing DTT, such as positive reinforcement, prompting/fading procedures, and shaping, will also be discussed in Chapter 5. Here is an example of a teacher, Mrs. Adams, using DTT to teach a student named Allison to turn the page of the book during read aloud:

Mrs. Adams: (*reads the page of the book to the class*) Turn the page, Allison. (*antecedent*)

Allison: (*no response*)

Mrs. Adams: Turn the page, Allison. (*points to the page and pushes the book closer to Allison*) (*antecedent with a prompt*)

Allison: (*turns the page*)

Mrs. Adams: (*smiles and makes eye contact with Allison*) Thank you, Allison. Look what happened now! (*consequence: positive reinforcement*)

Pivotal Response Training

PRT is another application of ABA that provides structured teaching within the child's natural environment (Koegel, Koegel, Harrower, & Carter, 1999). Unlike DTT, PRT focuses on addressing five pivotal areas as opposed to breaking skills down into discrete tasks. This is based on the premise that when these five pivotal areas are targeted, it leads to changes in other untargeted areas (Koegel & Koegel, 1995). The five pivotal areas include motivation, responsivity to multiple cues, self-management, self-initiations, and empathy (Koegel et al., 1999). PRT is typically used for early intervention with young children with ASD. Family involvement is a critical dimension because interventions are implemented across the child's day in natural contexts in the home and community. However, the general education classroom is also a natural environment that provides numerous learning opportunities throughout the day.

The PRT method can be used in the general education classroom by adapting the general education curriculum to include procedures for enhancing motivation and teaching students how to respond to multiple cues, manage their behavior, make initiations, and develop empathy for others. Strategies that are used when implementing PRT include making environmental arrangements in natural contexts to create opportunities for social interaction and communication, following the child's lead to increase motivation, and providing natural reinforcement for attempts made by the student (Koegel & Koegel, 2006). These strategies are discussed in detail in Chapter 5. Utilizing these strategies and implementing intervention in the natural environment helps to ensure that the skills being learned are generalized across a variety of contexts.

Here is an example of a teacher, Mr. Hart, using PRT in a general education classroom to teach a student named Alex how to point to a desired item:

Alex: (*stands next to the supply cabinet and whines as the students are lining up for recess*)

Mr. Hart: (*kneels down to get face-to-face with Alex; follows the student's lead*) You must want something, Alex.

Alex: (*continues to whine*)

Mr. Hart: Do you want that ball for recess? (*models how to point to the ball*)

Alex: (*reaches for the ball, but does not point*)

Mr. Hart: Here you go, Alex. (*gives Alex the ball as natural reinforcement and will work on teaching Alex to point instead of reach next time*)

Incidental Teaching

IT is another application of ABA that uses natural contexts to promote the use of communication and social interaction (Hart & Risley, 1975). With IT, caregivers and teachers follow the child's lead to create opportunities for the child to communicate to get their needs and wants met. As is true with PRT, IT focuses on increasing initiations, enhancing motivation, and promoting generalization. Natural reinforcement, environmental arrangements, time delay, prompting/fading procedures, and modeling/request imitation are strategies that are used when implementing IT (see Chapter 5 for descriptions of these strategies). Typically developing peers can be taught how to use IT and PRT to promote communication and social interaction with children with ASD (McGee et al., 1992; Pierce & Schreibman, 1995, 1997). The use of peer-mediated interventions such as these is discussed in Chapter 5.

Applied Verbal Behavior

AVB is an application of ABA that incorporates DTT but also relies on B.F. Skinner's (1957) classification of language to teach language acquisition. This entails first teaching students with ASD to request, label, imitate, and then engage in conversations. Based on Skinner's work, the terms used for these skills in AVB are *mand, tact, echoic, intraverbal, textual,* and *transcriptive* (Sundberg & Michael, 2001). There are some additional differences between DTT and AVB that have been clearly explained in an article in *The Behavior Analyst Today* (Kates-McElrath & Axelrod, 2006). In DTT, children often engage in escape-motivated behavior, meaning they complete a task to get a break away from the task. With AVB, the interventionists establish themselves as conditioned social reinforcers. This means that the children are taught to enjoy the interactions they are having with the individual they are working with as opposed to always trying to get away from the interaction. Another difference between DTT and AVB is that whereas DTT is typically implemented in a one-to-one distraction-free environment, AVB includes intervention in the natural environment, or natural environment training, in addition to intervention in a distraction-free environment to enhance motivation. DTT and AVB use different curriculum guides for goal selection. DTT uses a curriculum developed by Lovaas and others as a scope and sequence (Lovaas, 2003; Lovaas et al., 1981; Maurice, Green, & Luce, 1996). AVB uses the *Assessment of Basic Language and Learning Skills* curriculum developed by Partington and Sundberg (1998). In general education classrooms, however, using these structured curriculum guides is not necessarily appropriate. Goals must be individualized, developmentally appropriate, and meaningful for the student within the general education classroom. Chapter 4 discusses goal selection in detail.

Chapter Summary

Although these different applications of ABA have been shown to make positive impacts on the learning of students with ASD, the research conducted was often not implemented in general education classrooms. The fact of the matter is that it is not practical for general education teachers to implement DTT, PRT, IT, or AVB in the same manner as was done in the studies that were conducted in settings outside of the general education classroom. Therefore, this book provides methods for implementing ABA in general education classrooms that address the guidelines presented by Baer et al. in 1968 and utilize the teaching procedures that have been shown to be effective by researchers who developed DTT, PRT, IT, and AVB. This is done by highlighting the actual teaching strategies that are used across these different intervention methods. In fact, many of the same behavioral strategies are used across all four teaching methods, some strategies are used with only two or three of the methods, and other teaching strategies may be specific to one method. However, if the strategies are presented as a whole, teachers can then develop technological teaching procedures utilizing strategies that have been shown to be effective by the various applications of ABA for students with ASD without having to select one specific teaching method. This book provides teachers with a method of implementing ABA in general education classrooms by presenting ways to select goals (applied); write objectives (behavioral); collect baseline and intervention data (analytic); develop clear, explicit teaching procedures that use behavioral strategies that have been shown to be effective (conceptual and technological); analyze the data to make instructional decisions (effective); and ensure that students learn how to use the acquired skills across a variety of situations and contexts (generality).

3

Assessment for Planning ABA Interventions

• •

The first step in designing ABA interventions for students with ASD in general education classrooms is to conduct and interpret assessments to gather specific information about the students' strengths and interests and present abilities. This chapter begins with a framework for conducting assessments to plan ABA interventions. Explanation for how these assessments can also be a part of the IEP planning process is provided. Assessment procedures for assessing the strengths and interests of students with ASD are discussed. To ensure goals are developmentally appropriate, it is important to assess the students' present levels of performance. Methods for assessing present levels of performance in communication, social interaction, academics, behavior, and independent functioning are included (see also Appendixes A–E). The chapter concludes with procedures for assessing parent priorities and general education teacher priorities to help set goals that are not only developmentally appropriate, but also meaningful across home, school, and community contexts.

Framework for Assessment

When planning ABA interventions for students with ASD in the general education classroom, it is crucial to conduct assessments before writing goals. As mentioned in Chapter 2, the assessments conducted will not be derived from commercially prepared curricula developed for specific ABA applications, such as DTT or AVB. Instead, informal assessments should be conducted to be able to develop interventions that are individualized and meaningful to the student within the context of the general education classroom. It is important to note that plans for use of ABA do not have to be separate from the IEP. The assessment procedures discussed in this chapter can certainly be used for developing the student's IEP. On the other hand, not every goal on the IEP requires the use of ABA intervention. Typically, the objectives selected for the development of ABA interventions are the ones that the student is not making adequate progress toward mastering. What is important, though, is to conduct quality assessments before aligning objectives for ABA interventions to ensure they are developmentally appropriate for the student. Teachers can determine that the student is ready to learn the objectives set forth because of the information gained during the assessment process. This chapter focuses on procedures for assessing the student's strengths and interests; the student's present levels of performance in communication, social interaction, academics, behavior, and independent functioning; and parent and teacher priorities.

Assessing the Strengths and Interests of the Student

Most IEPs have a small section to indicate the strengths and interests of the student. Usually a sentence or two is written to meet the requirement, and this information is then left on the back burner. IEP objectives are written and teaching procedures are implemented, often without considering the strengths and interests of the student. Although addressing the strengths and interests of all students is important, it is especially important for students with ASD. These students are often asked to engage in activities that they find difficult and that they do not enjoy. Because of their impairments in communication and social interaction, many everyday tasks that are challenging for all students are even more difficult for students with ASD. Also, many students with ASD have a restricted range of interests, making it less likely that they will have motivation to engage in a variety of different activities. One way to increase motivation, however, is to assess a student's strengths and interests so they can be considered when setting goals and then also embedded into learning activities (Bianco, Carothers, & Smiley, 2009). It is important to find out what the student's strengths and interests are so that they can be accessed and built upon to enhance future learning and increase motivation. Strengths are things that the student is good at, whereas interests are things the student likes. Assessments can be performed by interviewing the student, parents, teachers, other professionals, and paraprofessionals and by conducting preference assessments through direct observation in the classroom.

Interviews

One of the most effective ways to find out about the student's strengths and interests is to conduct interviews. These interviews also assist teachers in starting out the annual IEP process in a positive, collaborative manner and help parents and professionals focus on the positive aspects of the student. It is very easy for parents and professionals to highlight all the areas of need and deficits of the student, but it is often not as easy for them to discuss the strengths and interests of the student. Having a positive framework does wonders for promoting developmental gains in students. Figure 3.1 provides a list of questions that can be asked to a student, and Figure 3.2 provides a list of questions that can be asked to parents or teachers and other school staff members. The questions provided do not all necessarily need to be asked. They serve as possible probing questions if the student, parent, or teacher cannot think of a variety of strengths and interests.

Opening statement	Student response
Tell me about your strengths and interests.	I am good at reading. I love animals.
Additional probing questions	**Student response**
What types of things do you like?	Dinosaurs, reptiles, zoos
What are you good at?	I read fast and I can read big words. I know a lot of facts about different animals.
What makes you happy?	When people are nice to me
What are your favorite toys?	Animal figurines, magazines about animals
What do you like to do?	Go places like zoos, museums, and the library
Who do you like to spend time with?	My mom, my little brother
What are your favorite times of the day?	After dinner
What can you do that many other kids cannot do?	Remember lots of stuff about animals
What are your favorite places?	(indicated this already)
What are some things in your house or school that you would never want to give up?	DVDs, dinosaur toys, magazines

Figure 3.1. Assessing strengths and interests: student interview.

Date	Student's name	Interviewer	Individual responding
9/16/09	Jordan Smith	Lauren Jones (general education teacher)	Lisa Smith (mother)

Opening statement	Parent/teacher response
Tell me about the student's strengths and interests.	Jordan loves anything that has to do with animals.

Additional probing questions	Parent/teacher response
What makes the student happy?	Playing with his animal figurines
How does the student prefer to spend his or her time?	He likes to play with his figurines by himself, flip through pages of magazines about animals, and watch DVDs about animals.
What are the student's favorite toys or activities?	(indicated in previous questions)
In what areas does the student excel?	Reading; he can read just about anything you put in front of him.
What about the student makes you proud?	He is loving, I am proud that he can read so well, and I am proud that he can remember a lot of factual information.
Who does the student like to spend time with?	Mostly me
What are the student's favorite times of the day?	Before he takes a shower at night when I sit in his room while he plays with his figurines
What keeps the student's attention?	Movies, pictures, objects
What are the student's favorite places?	Library, Target, zoo, children's museum
What would the student never want to give up?	His animal figurines, his books and magazines about animals, and his DVDs

Figure 3.2. Assessing strengths and interests: parent/teacher interview.

Preference Assessments

If a student with ASD cannot verbally communicate to indicate strengths and interests, *preference assessments* can be conducted to allow the student to share this information. Preference assessments help teachers identify potentially reinforcing items, activities, or contexts by having the student make selections between two or more alternatives (Layer, Hanley, Heal, & Tiger, 2008). For example, if you want to determine what

Student's name		Individual conducting assessment	
Ben		Martha (general educator)	
Date/activity	Choice 1	Choice 2	Selection
9/05: Language arts vocabulary activity	Sports list (shown pictures)	Transportation list (shown pictures)	Transportation list
9/05: Math addition activity	Add with pretzels	Add with matchbox cars as counters	Matchbox cars
9/06: Silent reading activity	Book about transportation	Book about Spider-Man	Book about transportation
9/06: Science center	Use magazine pictures of animals to create examples of adaptations	Use magazine pictures of modes of transportation to create examples of different ways to travel	Transportation activity

Figure 3.3. Preference assessment recording form.

snacks a student prefers, you can systematically offer choices and document what the student selects. You can offer popcorn or chocolate and indicate the selection. If the student selects popcorn, you can then offer popcorn or crackers and indicate the selection. It is best to do this type of assessment over the course of several days to best determine the true preferences of the student. You can do the same thing with activity preferences by presenting choices of activities such as working on the computer, participating in the art center, playing basketball, or any other option for activities in the classroom and the school. The same process can be conducted for academic preferences. You can offer choices of academic activities such as math facts sheets, books to read, audio tapes to listen to, or materials for writing. By conducting these preference assessments, teachers can find out the strengths and interests of a student through direct observation. Of course, preferences will change over time, so these assessments should be conducted again if the student seems to be developing different preferences. Figure 3.3 provides a sample recording form for conducting preference assessments.

Assessing to Determine Present Levels of Performance

Present levels of performance are statements that indicate what a student can currently do in a given domain that allow teachers to then create goals that are developmentally appropriate. The key word is *can* do. It is very easy to make a list of all of the things a student cannot do, but that does not necessarily help in determining objectives that are developmentally appropriate. Assessments must be systematically planned and conducted to allow teachers to indicate exactly what a student is able to do. For students with ASD, it is absolutely necessary to assess present levels of performance in communication and social interaction, because these are their core deficit areas that require intervention. Most students with ASD will need goals developed in the areas of academics, behavior, and independent functioning as well. Often, formal assessments do not give adequate information because the communication and social deficits of students with ASD impede their ability to demonstrate skills they have acquired. Although some standardized, formal assessments can be helpful in determining present levels of performance, this chapter will present a variety of supplemental informal assessments that teachers can use to get an accurate picture of what the student can do.

Assessing Communication Skills

Communication skills can be assessed through formal, standardized language assessments and through parent and teacher interviews and direct observation in the classroom and other school settings. Both interviewing and direct observation are recommended to gather enough information about the student's communication skills. Although there are countless skills that fall under the domain of communication, it is important to remember that with ABA programming, goals that have meaning and can make the most positive impact on the child's success in the general education classroom should be chosen. It is true that a goal for a student such as knowing multiple meanings of words may be developmentally appropriate; however, if the student cannot engage in a reciprocal conversation with peers, a goal related to conversational skills may be more meaningful (or applied, if we consider the components of ABA presented in Chapter 2). With that said, teachers can benefit from resources such as Kathleen Quill's book, *Do-Watch-Listen-Say* (2000), which provides comprehensive information for assessing communication skills. Tools such as the ones provided in Quill's book are useful for providing a scope and sequence for communication skills. However, school-based teams must use their best judgment in selecting goals that are the most meaningful for the student when developing ABA intervention programs. In fact, sometimes communication goals that are not even listed on scope and sequence checklists can be developed for students if the skills are necessary for successful inclusion in the general education classroom.

Figure 3.4 provides an informal assessment tool that teachers can use to assess communication skills for students with ASD. The tool provides specific questions to ask during the interview process and then a place to document additional information gained through direct observation. Again, this is not an exhaustive list of all possible communication skills that a student can and should learn. These are essential skills that students with ASD often have difficulty with that negatively impact their learning and socialization opportunities if not addressed through intervention. When documenting on the form, list what the student can do as opposed to what the student cannot do. For example, you may indicate that the student can follow one-step

Student's name	Sarah	
Question	**Information gathered from interviews**	**Information gathered from direct observation** (general education classroom)
How does the student express wants and needs?	Mother: She pulls me to bring me to what she wants; she cries. General education teacher: She cries, whines, grabs.	During recess, Sarah grabbed a ball out of a student's hand. During lunch, Sarah whined until the assistant came over. The assistant helped her open her drink.
How does the student express frustration or anger?	Mother: Walks away, cries, yells General education teacher: Displays off-task behaviors, whines, may leave the work area	During centers, Sarah was working at the literacy center. She had trouble using the letter stamps. She quickly left that center to choose another one.
What types of directions can the student follow? (Consider one-step, multistep, simple, complex, academic, behavioral, social.)	Mother: Many one-step directions and even some multistep directions Teacher: Most one-step directions I give as long as I give them to her individually. When I give directions to the whole class, she often cannot follow them.	During whole-group instruction, each time the teacher gave a direction to the class, Sarah was unable to follow the direction. However, when the teacher approached Sarah one-to-one and restated the direction, she was able to comply.
What types of questions can the student answer/ ask? (Consider questions about academic content, common knowledge, the past, recent or very recent past, ongoing activities, the future, personal information.)	Mother: What is it? Teacher: Simple questions about common objects such as "What is it?" and "What do you see?"	During read aloud, Sarah was able to answer questions about the pictures in the book to include: "What animal is this?" and "What is he eating?"
What types of comments does the student respond to/initiate? (Consider comments made during academic activities and social activities.)	Mother: none Teacher: none	Did not observe Sarah initiating any comments. Peers made a few comments to Sarah during a group activity, but she did not respond.
To what level can the student engage in conversation with adults/peers? (Consider topics, length of back-and-forth exchanges, ability to initiate conversations, join conversations, end conversations, remain on topic.)	Mother: She does not engage in conversation. Teacher: She does not engage in conversation.	Did not observe Sarah engage in any type of conversation.

Figure 3.4. Assessing communication skills.

directions with maximum teacher prompting instead of saying the student cannot follow directions. Examples of ways that students may communicate that can be indicated on the assessment tool may include the following:

1. Whining/crying/screaming

2. Aggression (hitting oneself or others; destroying property)

3. Grabbing, reaching or pulling a person to desired items

4. Gestures (pointing, nodding/shaking head, waving)

5. Making eye contact

6. Imitation (imitate gestures/sounds/words)

7. Initiating verbalizations (single sounds; one-word, two-word, simple, or complex sentences; or asking questions)

8. Actions (when responding to directions/comments or initiating interactions)

9. Writing/typing

10. Using an augmentative communication device

11. Using pictures

Assessing Social Interaction Skills and Social Skills

Many researchers and practitioners have different definitions for the terms *social skills* and *social interaction skills.* In this book, social interaction skills are referred to as the skills required for individuals to develop meaningful relationships with others. Students with ASD typically have deficits in social interaction skills because of their limited joint attention skills and social reciprocity skills (see Chapter 1). Thus, when assessing social interaction skills, the focus will be on assessing joint attention and social reciprocity. Social skills are referred to as specific skills individuals need to learn to avoid social failure and rejection. These skills are often the "hidden curriculum" in schools (Myles & Simpson, 2001; Myles, Trautman, & Schelvan, 2004). In other words, these are the skills that most typically developing children learn incidentally without explicit instruction. Figure 3.5 provides a tool for assessing social interaction skills. Just like the tool provided for assessing communication skills, there is one place for recording information based on teacher or parent interview and one place for recording information based on direct observation. Figure 3.6 provides a tool for assessing social skills. For each skill, indicate whether the student displays that skill independently or whether prompting is needed. If prompting is needed, in the space provided, specifically indicate the level of prompting needed. The more specific teachers are in the descriptions, the easier it will be to create developmentally appropriate goals. The skills listed are simply examples of social skills that students with ASD often have difficulty with. However, there are many other

Student's name	Blake	
Question	Information gathered from interviews	Information gathered from direct observation (general education classroom)
What is the student's ability to respond to joint attention bids from others? (Consider whether the student allows others to join in on what the student is currently engaged with; consider whether the student responds to comments, directions, or questions made by others verbally and/or nonverbally.)	Parents: Blake is usually okay with it when others join his play. He usually just does his own thing while the other child plays next to him. General education teacher: When other children join Blake, he seems to be happy with that. When peers make comments or ask him questions, he answers only some of the time.	During recess, Blake was playing with the steering wheel on the play structure. Another student came up to Blake and started spinning the steering wheel with him. Blake remained engaged in the activity. The student said, "Let's drive to the movies!" Blake did not respond.
What is the student's ability to maintain joint attention with others? (Consider duration of time, types of activities.)	Parents: Blake can play alongside other kids for about 5 minutes most of the time. General education teacher: There are times when Blake will remain in an activity alongside a peer for 5 minutes or so, but usually after 1 or 2 minutes he moves on to another activity. He plays alongside peers the longest when they are playing with constructive play toys.	During partner reading, Blake engaged in a book with a peer by holding the book and turning the pages. The peer made comments about the pictures on each page. Blake did not look at the peer or use any verbalizations throughout the activity.
What is the student's ability to initiate joint attention with others? (Consider verbal and nonverbal initiations, types of activities that stimulate initiations.)	Parents: Blake will often bring us his favorite toys. He likes for us to help him get started building a Lincoln Log house. General education teacher: Blake hardly makes any initiations with peers or adults. One time, however, a student was looking at a book that Blake likes, and Blake sat down next to the student.	No observations of initiations on Blake's part were observed.

Figure 3.5. Assessing social interaction skills.

(continued)

Figure 3.5. *(continued)*

Student's name	Blake	
Question	**Information gathered from interviews**	**Information gathered from direct observation** (general education classroom)
To what extent can the student engage in reciprocal social interactions with peers/adults? (Consider length of back-and-forth verbal and/or nonverbal interactions; consider social and academic activities.)	Parents: This is very difficult for Blake. General education teacher: Blake cannot easily engage in back-and-forth interactions, but he is able to engage in some simple back-and-forth interactions with me if I use lots of prompting to help him respond.	During centers, the teacher joined Blake at the science center. She picked up a magnet and said, "This is cool!" Blake looked at the magnet and reached for it. The teacher held the magnet back and said, "Do you want to hold it?" Blake said, "Yes." The teacher gave the magnet to Blake.

Student's name	Gabriel	
Skill	**Independent**	**Level of prompting needed**
Shares materials during joint tasks	X	
Shares materials during independent/parallel tasks	X	
Responds when others offer a turn	X	
Offers a turn to others		If a peer says, "It's my turn," and puts out a hand as a prompt, Gabriel will usually give the peer a turn.
Maintains attention while waiting for a turn		Gabriel usually requires extensive prompting to remain engaged while waiting his turn.
Offers help to others		If the teacher says something such as "Brandon needs help with cleaning up," Gabriel will usually help.
Accepts help from others	X	
Empathizes with the feelings of others		Gabriel needs verbal prompts to recognize the feelings of others and to respond appropriately.

Figure 3.6. Assessing social skills.

Figure 3.6. *(continued)*

Uses appropriate voice volume		Gabriel often needs prompts to talk loud enough for others to hear him.
Uses appropriate space with a social partner	X	
Responds to greetings	X	
Initiates greetings		Gabriel needs verbal prompts such as, "Say hello to Adam."
Uses appropriate eye contact when interacting with others		When items are withheld briefly, Gabriel will usually establish eye contact to gain access to the items.
Gives compliments to others		Gabriel can do this by imitating the words of the teacher.
Receives compliments positively	X	
Maintains personal hygiene	X	
Responds appropriately to facial expressions of others		Gabriel needs verbal prompts to read and respond appropriately to facial expressions.
Responds appropriately to body language of others		Gabriel needs verbal prompts to read and respond appropriately to the body language of others.
Appropriately responds when others are in the way		Gabriel will usually push his way through a situation. If the teacher says, "Say excuse me," he will imitate the expression.
Compromises during academic and social activities		Gabriel needs high levels of assistance when activities are not going the way he wants or had planned to avoid negative behaviors from occurring.

skills that may require assessment. There are some valuable resources available that provide a more comprehensive list of social skills that can be assessed for students with ASD. Kathleen Quill's book, *Do-Watch-Listen-Say* (2000), and Scott Bellini's book, *Building Social Relationships* (2006), both provide assessment tools that are useful for teachers when assessing social interaction skills and social skills.

Assessing Academic Skills

When it comes to informally assessing academics, most teachers have a good grasp on a variety of ways to accomplish this. However, with the current push toward standardized assessments, sometimes teachers lose sight of the valuable information that is gained through informal academic assessments that cannot necessarily be obtained with standardized measures. When considering students with ASD, this is especially true. Students with ASD often do not understand the expectations of standardized assessments and thus do not demonstrate what they are actually able to do. Their impairments in communication and social interaction require assessors to be creative and responsive to individual learning styles to gather information about what the students can truly do academically. The use of curriculum-based assessment, performance assessment, portfolio assessment, and authentic assessment enable teachers to obtain information about a student's achievement or performance, identifying both strengths and needs of the student (Daniels, 1999; Hargrove, Church, Yssel, & Koch, 2002).

Teachers must remember that the student's communication skills will have an impact on academic performance. For example, reading comprehension cannot be assessed without also assessing and considering communication skills. If a student cannot answer simple conversational questions, the student is going to have difficulty answering comprehension questions from reading material. Therefore, communication assessment and academic assessment must go hand in hand, and then the communication goals and academic goals must be aligned. An example of alignment between a communication goal and a reading comprehension goal is as follows:

- *Communication goal:* The student will be able to respond to simple conversational questions about recent activities by providing at least a one-word response 80% of the time.

    Examples: What did you eat for lunch? Where did your dad take you? Who got hurt at recess?

- *Reading comprehension goal:* The student will be able to respond to simple literal questions pertaining to reading material at the first-grade level by providing at least a one-word response 80% of the time.

    Examples: Where did the family go on vacation? What did the boy see at the park? Who fell off the bed?

When selecting academic goals for ABA programming, select goals that the student is having difficulty mastering with other classroom teaching procedures. It may be that the student requires more explicit instruction to achieve the IEP goal than the student is currently receiving. Often assessments must be done to determine whether the student has the prerequisite skills required for the specific goal that is on the IEP. Even if the goal is developmentally appropriate in that the student should be able to master it over the course of a year, the skills the student needs to learn before achieving the annual goal may require explicit ABA interventions. After that is done, objectives can be developed for ABA interventions based on what the student is currently able to do and what skills are needed to enable the student to move toward mastery of the IEP goal. Figure 3.7 provides an example of how academic assessment results can be recorded.

Student's name	Hannah	
Academic area	Results from formal/ standardized assessments	Results from informal assessments
Reading (Consider phonemic awareness, phonics, fluency, comprehension, and vocabulary.)	Results from the Diagnostic Achievement Battery 3 (DAB-3) indicate that Hannah is in the 5th percentile for broad reading. She performed the highest on the alphabet/word knowledge subtest and the lowest on reading comprehension.	Hannah can identify all letters by name and knows their corresponding sounds. She can phonetically sound out C-V-C words. She can read fluently at a kindergarten level. Hannah can answer literal comprehension questions based on material read aloud to her at the first-grade level. Hannah needs extensive support to define key terms in text.
Math (Consider number concepts, computations, application, and problem solving.)	Results from the DAB-3 indicate that Hannah is in the 25th percentile for broad math. She performed the highest on the math calculation subtest and the lowest on math reasoning.	Hannah mastered rote memorization of basic addition facts. She can compute basic subtraction facts using manipulatives with some teacher support. Hannah needs extensive teacher assistance to solve simple word problems. Hannah can tell time to the hour and half hour. Hannah knows the names of all coins.
Language arts (Consider listening, speaking, and writing.)	No standardized measures used.	Hannah is able to request desired items and activities using simple sentences. She answers some basic questions related to present activities and the very recent past. She will ask for help if she needs assistance. Hannah needs extensive teacher assistance to write words.
Content area (Consider how students learn new concepts and vocabulary, participation in whole-group and small-group instruction, cooperative learning activities, and independent work.)	No standardized measures used.	Hannah is able to grasp concrete concepts when engaged in hands-on learning experiences. She can answer basic questions related to the content during these types of activities. Hannah needs extensive supports to learn key vocabulary terms related to content area concepts.

Figure 3.7. Assessing academic skills.

Assessing Behavior

When students with ASD display behavioral challenges in the general education classroom, teachers must consider the function for these behaviors before developing ABA interventions. Some teachers may say that a student displays a certain behavior for no reason at all. However, all challenging behaviors serve a purpose, whether the student has ASD or not. It is important to understand this because the purpose the behavior serves should lead to specific interventions. For example, if a student shouts out during whole-group instruction for the purpose of getting negative attention from the teacher, the teacher would need to refrain from giving negative attention when the student calls out. Instead, the interventions would need to focus on increasing positive attention when the student is engaging in appropriate behaviors. On the other hand, if the student shouts out because the student is not engaged in the instructional activities, the teacher would need to focus on adjusting the lesson to increase active engagement for the student.

Teachers can informally assess through direct observation and interviewing to determine the purpose that the challenging behavior serves. There is a wealth of literature in support of conducting functional behavioral assessments to develop behavioral intervention plans that readers can refer to for more information (Hanley, Piazza, Fisher, & Maglieri, 2005; Horner, 1994; O'Neill et al., 1997; Scott & Caron, 2005; Sugai et al., 1999). When conducting functional behavior assessments with students with ASD, however, it is important to consider their core deficits in social interaction and communication. Because students with ASD have difficulty establishing positive relationships and communicating with others, they may engage in challenging behaviors to get their social and communication needs met and to express their frustration, anxiety, or lack of engagement. This is important for teachers to understand, because behavioral intervention plans are often developed to simply attempt to reduce problem behaviors such as self-stimulatory behavior, noncompliance, off-task behavior, or aggression. But the fact of the matter is that if teachers do not get to the root of the problem and provide students with a positive replacement behavior that meets their needs, they will end up playing a game of Whac-A-Mole in which they stop or reduce one behavior only to see that a different challenging behavior pops up. Therefore, it is important to assess what the student is having difficulty communicating, what the student is trying to gain socially, and what the student may be feeling anxious about, frustrated with, or disengaged from.

Figure 3.8 provides an assessment tool that can be used in conjunction with other functional behavioral assessment resources to address specific behavioral issues related to working with students with ASD in general education classrooms. There are four possible hypotheses listed. These are just some common functions for challenging behavior of students with ASD. Of course, there can be many other hypotheses. For each hypothesis, there is a place to record data based on interviews, direct observation, and functional analysis. Functional behavioral assessment interviews are commonly conducted with parents, teachers, and other school staff to gather as much information as possible about the possible functions for the challenging behavior. On the form provided, teachers can summarize the information

Name of student	Name of assessor		
Max	Wanda (special educator)		
Hypothesis	Data collected through interview	Data collected through direct observation	Data collected through functional analysis
To communicate wants and needs	General educator indicated that Max screams if he wants something and doesn't know how to ask for it.	In the cafeteria, Max started screaming. The assistant went over and noticed that Max needed a straw for his milk. She gave him the straw and he stopped screaming.	(none)
To communicate frustration or anxiety due to skill deficit	General educator indicated that he doesn't typically ask for help if he needs it, but instead he will start screaming.	During a variety of independent work activities and group lessons, Max would scream. The teacher would come over to help him, and he would stop screaming.	When Max was given easy tasks to complete, he did not scream. When he was actively engaged in a lesson, he did not scream.
To gain social attention/ interaction	(none)	(none)	(none)
To gain engage-ment or avoid disengagement/ boredom	The general education teacher indicated that when Max is not engaged in the lessons going on in the classroom, he will often scream intermit-tently throughout the lesson.	During a math lesson on determining the perimeter of a shape, Max was not raising his hand to answer questions and was not called on throughout the lesson. He screamed loudly several times, often smiling while screaming.	During a hands-on science lesson related to gravity, Max did not scream. He was actively engaged in the activities requiring him to work in a team to test out which items would fall the fastest.

Figure 3.8. Assessing problem behavior.

gained from these interviews into any of the possible hypotheses. There may be, and often is, more than one function for challenging behavior of students with ASD. Therefore, information gained from an interview may be placed in more than one section if a student seems to have more than one function for the challenging behavior. For example, a student may engage in aggression toward peers when they attempt to join the student in play to try to avoid social interactions. The same student may also engage in aggression toward peers to get attention from the peers or teachers. For each hypothesis, there is also a place to record data based on direct observation. This can be A-B-C data, scatterplot data, anecdotal data, or any other data gained through actual classroom observations. A-B-C data entail documenting what happens right before the behavior occurs, a description of the behavior, and what happens after the behavior occurs. Scatterplot data entail recording the frequency of the target behavior during different times of the day to determine when the behavior is most and least likely to occur. Anecdotal data entail writing descriptive notes when a challenging behavior occurs that may provide information related to the function for the behavior. Finally, there is a place to indicate data collected during a functional analysis. These are data that are collected when variables in the environment are manipulated to test out a specific hypothesis. For example, if it is hypothesized that a student engages in self-injurious behaviors when presented with difficult tasks, teachers can provide easy tasks and document the student's reaction and then provide more challenging tasks and document to determine the differences in behavior when easy or difficult tasks are presented.

Assessing Independent Functioning Skills

Independent functioning refers to many different skills. This domain includes activities of daily living, organizational skills, motor skills, independent play skills, and attention-related skills. Activities of daily living may include things such as potty training, eating independently, or tying shoes. Organizational skills may include skills such as organizing materials, turning in assignments, or placing incomplete assignments in the appropriate place. Motor skills may include skills such as handwriting, throwing a ball back and forth, or cutting with scissors. Independent play skills may include playing appropriately with a variety of age-appropriate toys or playing for a certain period of time independently. Attention-related skills may include skills such as staying on task to complete academic assignments, attending to the teacher during group instruction, or transitioning from one activity to another. Of course, these are all just examples of skills that could be assessed within the domain of independent functioning. There are many other skills for which a student may require intervention in each of these areas.

When assessing independent functioning skills, teachers can use formal adaptive behavior assessments, but often those assessments simply tell you what skills the child has and does not have. Therefore, you can use those as a starting place and then conduct more specific informal assessments for the skills on which you want to focus. This can be done by using *task analysis*. Simply take each skill that will be assessed and break it down into sequential steps. Then you can observe the student demonstrating the skill in order to learn which steps the student can currently do independently and which steps the student needs to learn, and you can set goals accordingly. Figure 3.9 shows a task analysis example for using the bathroom independently. This type of task analysis can also be done for a variety of other independent functioning

Step	Independent	Minimal prompting	Moderate prompting	Maximum prompting
1. Indicate the need to use the bathroom.				
2. Go into the bathroom and shut the door.				
3. Remove necessary clothing.				
4. Use the toilet.				
5. Wipe with toilet paper.				
6. Flush.				
7. Put clothing back on.				
8. Wash hands.				

Figure 3.9. Task analysis: using the bathroom independently.

skills. Notice that the assessment tool allows the teacher to document the level of prompting the student needs to demonstrate the specific skill. If the student completes the step without assistance, *independent* is checked. If the student requires very little assistance, *minimal prompting* is checked. If the student requires quite a bit of assistance, *moderate prompting* is checked. If the student requires constant assistance and/or hand-over-hand assistance, *maximum prompting* is checked. In this manner, teachers can easily track student skills, progress, and the effectiveness of supports.

Assessing Parent and General Education Teacher Priorities

After conducting formal and informal assessments across the domains appropriate for the student, determine parent and teacher priorities for intervention. Although you can do this in a more global way before conducting assessments to determine the particular areas on which to focus the assessments, it is best to get specific priorities set after the assessments. That way, the priorities can be based on what the student can presently do. This sets the team up for developing goals that are developmentally appropriate. After presenting assessment information, a good question to ask parents to assess their priorities is, "Based on what your child is currently able to do, what would you like to see your child do next?" This allows parents an opportunity to express their main priorities in a positive manner. When asked what their priorities are, parents often say things such as, "I want my child to stop _____." Or, they may say more broad things such as, "I just want my child to be happy." By first presenting assessment information and guiding parents to think about their child's present level of performance, specific parent priorities that are appropriate and realistic for the student are more likely to be shared.

Special education teachers are often responsible for assessing priorities of the general education teacher. The same process can be used that is used for assessing parent priorities. After presenting the assessment information, ask the teacher something such as, "Based on what the student can currently do and what skills are required for successful inclusion in the general education classroom, what would you like to see the student learn next?" This is important for teachers because sometimes goals are set that are not developmentally appropriate for the student simply because it is a general expectation for all students in the classroom. Although it is crucial to consider classroom expectations, the student's present level of performance must also be considered so that achievable goals are set. To get to point Z, we must go through A, B, C, D, and so forth. Therefore, if a teacher would like to see the student work independently for 45 minutes, but the assessment indicates the student can only work independently for 2 minutes, an appropriate goal to start with may be for the student to work independently for 5 minutes. Eventually the student may get to point Z (45 minutes), but that is more likely to be achieved by increasing the expectations for the student in smaller increments.

Chapter Summary

Before developing ABA interventions for students with ASD in general education classrooms, it is important to conduct assessments such as the ones discussed in this chapter. This allows teachers to determine the student's present level of performance across a variety of domains, which leads to the development of goals that are appropriate and meaningful for the student. It is important to include assessments of student strengths and interests so that they can be considered when setting goals and planning interventions. Depending on the needs of the student, you may assess present levels of communication skills, social interaction skills, academic skills, behavior, and/or independent functioning skills. Once present levels of performance are determined, assessment of parent and teacher priorities should be conducted to assist with goal setting. Once these assessments are completed and interpreted, intervention can be planned that will make the most positive impact on the student's success in the general education classroom.

4

Goal Setting

. . . .

Setting goals is the foundation of all education planning. For ABA interventions to be effective in the general education classroom, goals must be set on the basis of information gathered through assessments. These goals should be set in a collaborative manner with all team members, functional, developmentally appropriate, observable, and measurable; should indicate a criteria for mastery; and should be positively stated. This chapter includes examples of what are and are not appropriate goals. It also includes explanations of how you can link ABA interventions to IEP goals and objectives and how you can use ABA interventions to address behaviors and skills that may not be on an IEP.

Collaborative Goal Setting

When selecting goals for ABA intervention programs that will be implemented in general education classrooms for students with ASD, it is important for families, general education teachers, special education teachers, speech-language pathologists, and other related services professionals to work collaboratively. All too often, when developing IEP goals for these students, the speech-language pathologist writes the communication goals, and the special education teacher writes the social goals, behavioral goals, academic goals, and independent functioning goals, with little involvement from other team members. This is a big problem when it is time to implement the IEP in the general education classroom because the goals may not relate to that setting. The goals may be more clinical in nature if the speech-language pathologist and special education teacher write them with the intention of implementing intervention in pull-out sessions. Whether developing IEP goals, goals for ABA interventions, or both, it is crucial for the entire team to work together to create goals that are meaningful in the general education setting, address parent and teacher priorities, and are developmentally appropriate. Effective use of assessment (see Chapter 3) makes collaborative goal setting much easier because the team is aware of the student's strengths and interests, the student's present level of performance across a variety of domains, and the parents' and general education teachers' priorities. Then it becomes a matter of using that information, as a group, to develop goals based on assessment results.

Criteria for Writing Goals

Whether the goals are being written for IEPs, ABA interventions, or both, there are certain criteria that must be met. Federal law states that IEP goals must be functional, developmentally appropriate, observable, and measurable (IDEA, 2004). Goals should also indicate criteria for mastery and be positively stated. Each of these requirements are discussed in detail in the sections that follow and are summarized in Table 4.1.

Functional

If a goal is functional, it is meaningful for the student and will make a positive impact on the student's life when achieved. This is directly related to the *applied* dimension of ABA (Baer, Wolf, & Risley, 1968). If goals are clinical in nature, they may not be very meaningful for students. For example, a goal that states, "Shannon will match three-dimensional objects to pictures," is probably not a functional goal for many students. A good way to determine whether a goal is functional is to ask the "so what?" question. If the student masters the goal, so what? How will this new skill positively impact the student's life? If the question cannot be answered in a meaningful way, it is probably not a functional goal. Therefore, instead of teaching Shannon to match objects to pictures, it may be more meaningful to teach her to receptively identify common objects in the natural environment, in pictures, and in videos. If she can learn to identify common objects through pointing to them, then she can use that skill for a variety of communication, social, and academic needs. Shannon can then learn to request by pointing to desired objects or pictures of desired objects. Later, this skill can help enhance her participation during academic and social activities by

Table 4.1. Criteria for writing goals

Criterion	Description
Functional	The goal is meaningful for the student and appropriate for the general education classroom.
Developmentally appropriate	The goal is based on the present level of performance of the student.
Observable	The goal is stated to allow individuals to see the student demonstrating the skill. The expectation should be very clear so that all individuals are observing the same thing.
Measurable	The goal is stated so that it will be measured the same way by all individuals.
Indicates criteria for mastery	The goal includes the measurement required to demonstrate that it has been achieved by the student.
Positively stated	The goal states the skill(s) the student is expected to learn, not what the student should refrain from doing.

enabling her to point to pictures to indicate responses to questions and make comments to others.

Developmentally Appropriate

If a goal is developmentally appropriate, that means that the student is ready to learn what is stated. This is best determined by conducting a variety of assessments to develop a present level of performance of the student's current skills, as was discussed in Chapter 3. For example, a goal of "Michelle will respond appropriately to questions asked in class with five or more words using her augmentative communication device 80% of the time" would not be developmentally appropriate if she currently has only mastered yes or no responses on the device. However, this goal could be quite appropriate if Michelle sometimes responds with five or more words in class currently, or if she consistently demonstrates communication skills in other settings. Once the team has a clear understanding of the current skill set of the student across a variety of domains, the next step for each of the areas assessed would be developmentally appropriate goals.

Observable

A goal is observable if the teachers can actually see the student demonstrating the skill. This requirement of IDEA is directly linked to the *behavioral* dimension of ABA. A goal such as "Brian will enjoy recess" is not observable because teachers cannot see enjoyment. Enjoyment is not a particular behavior, and it often looks quite different for different individuals, especially if you consider some students with ASD who may not show positive affect much of the time. Instead, a goal can state that "Brian will play on the playground equipment, in the sandbox, or with items from the toy box for the majority of the recess period." Teachers can then observe whether or not the student is engaging in those play behaviors. Not only must teachers be able to see what the goal is stating, the goal must be written in such a way that a variety of individuals would be looking for exactly the same behaviors. The first example about the student enjoying recess would probably result in different individuals looking for different behaviors; however, the second example about playing on playground equipment, in the sandbox, or with toy box items lets all individuals know exactly what to look for.

Measurable and Indicates Criteria for Mastery

A goal is measurable if teachers can measure what they see the student doing and know the criteria for mastery (when the goal has been met). There should be something in the goal statement that indicates the type of measurement system that should be used. One common way that teachers indicate criterion for mastery is by indicating a percentage such as "Lucy will hand in her homework on time 90% of the time" or "Jewel will complete in-class math work with 80% accuracy." Although use of percentages can be a meaningful way to indicate mastery, it may not always be the most appropriate data collection method. For example, a goal of "Dennis will ask questions to his peers during cooperative learning activities" does not indicate how progress will be measured. However, if you add "independently" to the end, the goal is now measurable because the criteria for mastery is that Dennis will ask questions independently (or without teacher assistance). A level of independence rating system can be used to monitor progress (see Chapter 6). The example provided in the previous section about playing on the playground in the sandbox or with items from the toy box for the majority of the recess period is measurable because an individualized rating system can be developed to indicate the amount of time the student engaged in the behaviors indicated (none of the time, very little of the time, some of the time, the majority of the time). See Chapter 6 for additional ways to measure progress.

Table 4.2.   Sample goals for social interaction skills

Nonexample	Why the goal is a nonexample	Example	Why the goal meets criteria
The student will play with other children during recess 80% of the time.	This goal is too vague. Different individuals will have different meanings for the word "play." What the student is expected to do would have to be much more clearly defined. Recording the percentage of time a student is "playing" with other children is not realistic for a general education teacher to do during recess.	The student will respond to at least one request from a peer to play during each recess period by responding with positive verbalizations and/or actions for 5 consecutive school days.	The expectation is specific and can be observed and measured by all individuals the same way. The general education teacher can easily record whether the student meets the expectation during recess each day.
The student will participate in small-group academic and social games in the classroom given four out of five opportunities.	It is not clear what "participation" means for the student. Individuals can measure that quite differently.	The student will independently respond to comments and questions made by peers during small-group academic and social games in the classroom.	Participation is defined by responding to comments and questions for this student. Note that participation can be defined in many different ways as long as it is clear what is being measured. When the word *independently* is used in the goal, that means that data are going to be collected using a level of independence rating scale to indicate the amount of prompting required.

Positively Stated

Finally, goals should be positively stated. This helps teachers understand the skills that need to be taught to the student as opposed to just highlighting what the student cannot do. Academic standards are always stated positively, for example, "Students will demonstrate knowledge of how to graph linear functions," never negatively. A goal such as "Students will stop thinking that New York City is the capital of New York" seems ridiculous and offers little guidance on what exactly needs to be taught. Positively stated goals can also remind teachers to focus on what a student is good at, rather than reminding teachers why a student might frustrate them. For example, instead of writing "Justin will refrain from yelling out," write "Justin will raise a hand and wait quietly to be called on." If teachers only focus on reducing or eliminating behaviors, they usually are not getting to the root of the problem. Instead, goals should be set to teach new skills the student may need to replace the behavior that is undesirable.

Sample Goals

Tables 4.2–4.6 provide sample goals that meet the criteria stated above. The tables include nonexamples and examples, along with explanations to help you understand

Table 4.3. Sample goals for communication skills

Nonexample	Why the goal is a nonexample	Example	Why the goal meets criteria
The student will communicate wants and needs 80% of the time.	This goal is too vague. There are many different ways to communicate wants and needs, so that needs to be specified. Taking percentage data would not be appropriate because teachers don't necessarily know each time a student has a want or need and whether or not that was communicated appropriately each time.	The student will independently select a picture symbol from a field of 10 and give the picture symbol to an adult or peer to indicate specific wants and needs.	The expectation is specific and can be observed and measured by all individuals the same way. The general education teacher can record the level of prompting needed for the student to demonstrate the skill until independence is achieved.
The student will answer questions given three out of five opportunities.	There are a variety of different types of questions that students can be asked. The type of questions needs to be specified, as well as the context in which they are asked. Three out of five opportunities amount to only 60%. It would be better to set a goal at four out of five opportunities, or at least 80%.	The student will answer simple questions about present activities with 80% accuracy.	The type of questions is defined as simple questions and the context is present activities. Examples would be provided in the teaching procedures. They may include questions such as, "What are you making?" "Who is in the picture?" "Where do you write your name?"

Table 4.4. Sample goals for behavior

Nonexample	Why the goal is a nonexample	Example	Why the goal meets criteria
The student will remain on task 80% of the time.	This goal is too vague. There are many different ways that students can demonstrate on-task behavior, so that needs to be specified for this student. It would also need to be specified in what context(s) the student is expected to perform the expectation. It is quite difficult to document percentage for on-task behavior, so a level of independence or other rating system would be more appropriate.	The student will remain on task to complete at least 80% of assignments that are on the student's developmental level during independent work time.	The expectation is to remain on task, but it is demonstrated through task completion. It is quite easy to observe and record whether or not a student completed an assignment as opposed to whether or not the student was "on task." A general education teacher can easily document whether or not 80% of the assignments were turned in by using daily record keeping that is used for all students.
The student will refrain from rocking back and forth during instruction.	This goal is not stated positively. It only tells what the student shouldn't do as opposed to what the student should do. There is no criterion for mastery. Often if a student with ASD is engaging in stereotypic or self-stimulatory behavior during instructional activities, it is because they are disengaged. Thus the goal should focus on increasing engagement instead.	The student will participate in whole-group instruction by completing guided notes independently and answering at least two questions per lesson correctly.	The focus of the goal is on what behavior the student will engage in instead of rocking back and forth. The general education teacher can indicate whether or not the guided notes were completed and how many questions were answered correctly during each lesson.

Table 4.5. Sample goals for academics

Nonexample	Why the goal is a nonexample	Example	Why the goal is an appropriate example
The student will complete math problems with 100% accuracy.	This goal is too vague. There are many different types of math problems. Also, it is important to consider whether fluency is being expected or just accuracy.	The student will complete basic addition facts fluently with 100% accuracy.	The goal is specific to basic addition facts, and the criterion for mastery is that the student will be fluent and 100% accurate.
The student will learn new vocabulary.	This goal is too vague. It doesn't indicate what type of vocabulary will be learned, how learning will be measured, or how mastery will be determined.	The student will be able to draw pictures to demonstrate understanding of content area vocabulary words with 80% accuracy.	The expectation is clear (the student will draw pictures), the goal is related to content area vocabulary, and the criterion for mastery is set (80% accuracy).

Table 4.6. Sample goals for independent functioning

Nonexample	Why the goal is a nonexample	Example	Why the goal is an appropriate example
The student will keep assignments organized.	This goal is too vague. There are many different ways to keep assignments organized. It is not likely that all individuals would measure progress in the same way, and there is no criterion for mastery.	The student will place unfinished work in the designated folder and finished work in the designated basket with no more than two reminders per week.	The goal indicates how the student will organize assignments (use an unfinished work folder and the basket for completed work). It is measurable (indicate number of reminders needed per week) and has a criterion for mastery (no more than two reminders per week).
The student will be independent in the cafeteria each school day.	There are many ways that a student can be independent in the cafeteria. The goal would need to more specifically state the expectation.	The student will complete all of the steps for going through the lunch line independently each school day.	The expectation is clear (go through the lunch line independently). The goal suggests that a task analysis will be created, and the number of steps the student completes independently will be recorded.

the difference between goals that do not meet the criteria and those that do. Sample goals for social interaction skills, communication skills, behavior, academics, and independent functioning are given.

ABA Interventions for IEP Goals

ABA interventions can be quite useful to help students master IEP goals and objectives. That does not mean that all IEP goals for a student with ASD require ABA interventions, however. A good way to determine whether ABA interventions are necessary to help a student achieve IEP objectives is to measure the progress the student is making regularly. If the student is not making progress toward a specific objective, implementing ABA interventions targeting that objective would be a great way to boost progress. In some cases, ABA teaching procedures can be designed for the goal just as it is written on the IEP. In other cases, it would be more appropriate to break down the IEP goal or short-term objective into discrete skills the student needs to learn before addressing the actual IEP goal or objective. Consider an IEP goal that states, "Darren will independently greet the teacher and at least one peer each morning when arriving to school for five consecutive school days." Although this goal may be appropriate for Darren to achieve by the end of the school year, there may be several prerequisite skills that need to be taught first. He may first need to learn how to respond to greetings from the teacher, respond to greetings from peers, initiate teacher greetings, and initiate peer greetings before being able to independently greet the teacher and at least one peer each morning when arriving to school. Each of these subskills can be a goal for ABA teaching procedures.

ABA Interventions that Are Not Related to IEP Goals

When including students with ASD in general education classrooms, it is likely that there will be many skills and behaviors that are not necessarily on students' IEPs that nevertheless need to be explicitly instructed. For example, students may need ABA interventions to address behaviors related to participating in instructional activities, going through classroom routines, following classroom rules, turning in assignments, organizing materials, or making the transition between activities. Students with ASD may also require ABA interventions to address some "hidden curriculum" items. The hidden curriculum refers to the set of rules or guidelines that are often not directly taught but are assumed to be known (Hemmings, 2000), such as ways people indicate they wish to end a conversation. For the most part, typically developing students learn these social rules incidentally, but students with ASD often have difficulty understanding the hidden curriculum (Myles & Simpson, 2001) and require explicit instruction for many of these unwritten rules at school. For example, ABA interventions may be the most effective way to teach students appropriate bathroom, playground, hallway, and lunchtime behaviors (Myles, Trautman, & Schelvan, 2004).

There may also be some general education curriculum objectives that students need specialized instruction to learn that are not necessarily on their IEPs. These can include reading, writing, math, and content area standards that the students are not mastering with other classroom teaching procedures. The ABA interventions that can help the students, however, can occur as a part of the ongoing instruction in the classroom. For example, if a student is having difficulty answering inferential comprehension questions during read-aloud activities, ABA interventions can be developed and implemented during the usual read-aloud period to help the student learn this skill. The ABA teaching procedures would provide the teacher with additional strategies to include during the read-aloud activity, but would not be an additional lesson for the teacher to implement. For example, ABA teaching procedures may include using embedded discrete trials (see Chapter 5) to teach the student how to answer the comprehension questions. This would include providing prompts to help the student respond and positive reinforcement when the student does respond. The prompts would then be faded out until the student can respond independently. This type of instruction doesn't take anything away from the instruction of the other students. In fact, these same procedures can be used with typically developing students as well.

Chapter Summary

Goals for ABA interventions in the general education classroom should be developed on the basis of assessment information gathered, as was discussed in Chapter 3. These goals can address any of the following:

- Goals selected directly from the students' IEPs

- Prerequisite skills students need to learn to master IEP objectives

- Skills or behaviors to help the students actively participate in the general education classroom and meet behavioral expectations

- Hidden curriculum skills that students are not learning incidentally

- General education curriculum standards

After the goals are written, ABA teaching procedures are developed (see Chapter 5), and methods are selected for collecting and analyzing data to monitor progress and make instructional decisions (see Chapter 6).

5

Developing ABA Teaching Procedures

· ·

This chapter discusses methods for developing ABA teaching procedures that are conceptual and technological. Numerous behavioral strategies are explained in detail, including positive reinforcement, time delay, environmental arrangements, following the child's lead, self-monitoring, behavioral momentum, prompting/fading procedures, embedded discrete trials, modeling/request imitation, shaping, contingent imitation, balanced turn-taking, task analysis, video modeling, Social Stories, peer-mediated intervention, and direct instruction. The strategies are organized in two categories: strategies for increasing student performance for skills that they have but do not use fluently, consistently, or in a generalized manner and strategies for skill acquisition to teach students new behaviors and skills. The chapter concludes with a discussion for how to use a combination of these teaching strategies to develop ABA teaching procedures.

Developing Teaching Procedures

Chapter 1 discussed the seven dimensions of ABA presented by Baer, Wolf, and Risley in 1968. Chapter 4 discussed setting goals that are observable, measurable, developmentally appropriate, and functional, which addresses two of the seven dimensions: *applied* and *behavioral*. If goals are meaningful for students, parents, and teachers, the interventions are applied, and if they are also observable and measurable, they are behavioral. Two additional dimensions are addressed during the stage of developing teaching procedures: The procedures must be conceptual and technological. *Conceptual* means the teaching procedures include evidence-based strategies that have been shown to be effective through empirical behavioral research. There are a multitude of behavioral teaching strategies that can be included in ABA intervention plans. Several of these are discussed in this chapter. *Technological* means the teaching procedures are written in an explicit manner to ensure that all teachers implementing the intervention utilize the same method of instruction. This chapter discusses and includes examples of methods for creating teaching procedures that are conceptual and technological.

Behavioral Teaching Strategies

Many behavioral strategies that are considered part of the conceptual framework of ABA instruction are not new to teachers. Some strategies are widely known and used regularly with all students by most teachers. There are some strategies that teachers may use naturally that they do not necessarily know by the behavioral term, but they use them nonetheless. There are also a variety of strategies with which special education and general education teachers may not be familiar that are quite effective when working with students with ASD. The strategies selected for discussion in this chapter promote the use of positive behavioral interventions for students with ASD in general education classrooms. Punishment and behavior reduction are also behavioral strategies; however, the focus of this book is on using proactive and preventive ABA teaching procedures because they have been proven to more effectively promote positive behaviors and teach new skills (Scott & Caron, 2005; Sugai et al., 1999). This chapter presents 17 behavioral strategies that allow teachers to develop effective teaching procedures for just about any type of skill. When choosing strategies to use, it is important to consider whether skill performance is the main goal or whether skill acquisition is the main goal. If you are focusing on performance, the student actually has the skills required but is not using them fluently, consistently, or in a generalized manner. If you are focusing on skill acquisition, the student does not have the skills required to meet the expectations and requires explicit instruction. When performance is the issue, you can select strategies such as positive reinforcement, time delay, environmental arrangements, following the child's lead, self-monitoring, and behavioral momentum. When skill acquisition is the issue, you can select strategies such as prompting/fading procedures, embedded discrete trials, modeling/request imitation, shaping, contingent imitation, balanced turn-taking, task analysis, video modeling, social stories, peer-mediated intervention, and direct instruction. Remember, although it is not recommended that teachers choose a specific ABA approach such as DTT, PRT, IT, or AVB to implement in general education classrooms, it is important to recognize that the strategies discussed in this chapter all come from behavioral research, and many are used within these specific ABA approaches.

Positive Reinforcement

Positive reinforcement is a behavioral strategy that is often misinterpreted. Some teachers say they are providing positive reinforcement when they are actually providing repetition so the student can learn. For example, they may think they are providing positive reinforcement by providing many opportunities for a student to practice a specific academic skill, such as addition facts. That is actually positive practice, not positive reinforcement. Others may say that positive reinforcement does not work for their student. If that is the case, they are not providing positive reinforcement because the very definition of positive reinforcement suggests that it does work: Positive reinforcement entails delivering consequences after a behavior that increase the likelihood that the behavior will occur again in the future. Thus if teachers indicate that positive reinforcement is not working, they are actually saying that the consequences are not reinforcing for the student. The same types of things may not motivate students with ASD for a consistent period of time. They may have a strong desire for certain things one week, and the next week, have no interest in those same things at all. That is when conducting preference assessments can be quite helpful (see Chapter 3). It is important for teachers to understand, however, that there are many different types of positive reinforcement. These include tangible reinforcement, activity reinforcement, token reinforcement, social reinforcement, and natural reinforcement. Table 5.1 provides a description and examples for each of these types of reinforcement.

There is a misconception about students with ASD that they often require tangible and activity reinforcement to be motivated to complete tasks and meet expectations. However, this simply is not true. Students with ASD often respond very well to social reinforcement and natural reinforcement. If students are constantly presented with tasks that are difficult and boring, then yes, they will probably require tangible and activity reinforcers. However, when students are engaged in meaningful, interesting activities with the necessary supports to achieve success, social and natural reinforcements may be all that is needed.

Teachers should also be careful not to reinforce escape-motivated behaviors. If students are reinforced for completing a certain task or engaging in a certain activity by getting away from that very task or activity to do something else, students may learn to do something just to get away from it. So, in essence, reinforcing escape-motivated behaviors is the same as providing negative reinforcement: removing something unpleasant as a way of rewarding behavior. Instead of doing this, teachers should consider how they could make the activities themselves more reinforcing for the student and less aversive. It becomes quite difficult to build internal motivation when

Table 5.1. Positive reinforcement in the inclusive classroom

Reinforcer type	Example
Natural reinforcement	The student approaches a peer and asks to borrow a pair of scissors. The peer smiles, says, "Sure!" and hands the scissors to the student. The student is naturally reinforced to make requests such as this to peers in the future because the peer responded positively to the request, and the student obtained the desired item.
Social reinforcement	After the student completes an assignment independently, the teacher gets in close proximity to the student, establishes eye contact, smiles, and says, "Give me five! You did an awesome job!"
Token reinforcement	During whole-group instruction, the teacher gives stickers to the student each time the student volunteers to answer a question. When the student gets five stickers, they are traded in for a preferred activity or item.
Activity reinforcement	After the student reads a passage independently, the student is reinforced with computer time.
Tangible reinforcement	Each time the student completes a math problem, the student receives a pretzel stick.

external reinforcers are the main focus for the student. Thus building positive reinforcement into the activities themselves by making them interesting, fun, active, and socially reinforcing can promote more internal motivation for students.

Time Delay

The *time delay* strategy is often not used enough when working with students with ASD. Teachers are often quick to begin prompting a student if the student doesn't respond or initiate. This can cause students to get dependent on these prompts. To avoid prompt dependency, teachers can use time delay before prompting to allow opportunities for the students to respond without assistance (Halle, Marshall, & Spradlin, 1979). When using time delay, provide a short period of wait time paired with an expectant look and/or expectant body language. An expectant look can be a smile, raised eyebrows, or warm facial expressions. Expectant body language can include leaning in toward the student, shrugging shoulders, or putting hands up as if to say, "What?" It is important to be in close proximity to the student and at eye level when using time delay so the student learns to interpret the expectant looks and body language as invitations for a response or initiation. When teachers use time delay, it should be done in a positive, supportive manner to encourage the student to respond without fear of getting the answer wrong. If the student does not display an appropriate response or initiation after time delay is used, teachers can then use other strategies to ensure success.

Environmental Arrangements

Another effective strategy involves making *environmental arrangements* to promote communication and interaction (Koegel et al., 1999; McGee, Krantz, & McClannahan, 1985; Skokut, Robinson, Openden, & Jimerson, 2008). Four different environmental arrangement strategies can be used in general education classrooms to improve social interaction and communication skills for students with ASD. Teachers can place desired or needed items out of reach to provide opportunities for the student to make requests, give small amounts of desired or needed items to encourage the student to ask for more, do something unexpected to increase initiations from the student, or reduce environmental stimuli to limit distractions and prevent sensory overload. Table 5.2 provides examples for the four different types of environmental arrangements that can be used in the general education classroom.

Following the Child's Lead

Following the child's lead is a behavioral strategy that is used to increase communication and social skills. This strategy is one of the essential elements of PRT (Koegel et al., 1999) and IT (McGee, Morrier, & Daly, 1999). It entails beginning an interaction with a student by attending to what the student is doing at the time. To make

Table 5.2. Environmental arrangements in the inclusive classroom

Type of environmental arrangement	Example
Place desired items out of reach	If a student has a favorite book, put it high up on the bookshelf, making sure the student can still see it, to promote the use of social communication skills to request it.
Give small amounts of items	If a student is working on an assignment and needs a large quantity of a certain material, assign a peer in the classroom to be the one to give out that material. Teach the peer to give only a small amount at one time to provide many opportunities for the student to request more materials from the peer.
Do something unexpected	If the teacher or peer is walking with the student to the library, that person should purposefully go the wrong way to create an opportunity for the student to use social communication skills to correct the error.
Adjust environmental stimuli	If the student is working in a cooperative group with four students using many different math manipulatives to solve a problem and gets overwhelmed, adjust the group to only the student and one peer, and limit the amount of materials they are using to allow the student to attend to the task at hand without getting overloaded with too much sensory information.

following the child's lead an effective strategy, teachers should position themselves face-to-face with the child; present materials, actions, and objects that are interesting to the child; and make requests that are at the child's developmental level (Zanolli, Paden, & Cox, 1997). For example, if a student is playing with a ball at recess, the teacher or a peer joins the student and initiates joint play with the ball. The teacher or peer should get face-to-face with the student and provide opportunities for the student to engage successfully. If the student cannot throw the ball back and forth, do not begin the interaction that way. Instead encourage the student to roll the ball back and forth if the student is able to do that. The teacher or peer can also introduce different materials in which the student is interested to play with after the ball play.

The natural instinct of teachers when attempting to establish interactions between a student with ASD and a typically developing peer is often the opposite of following the child's lead. They may try to get the student to attend to what the peer is doing instead. When teachers do this, they end up fighting three battles at the same time: dealing with the student's social interaction difficulties, dealing with the difficulties that students with ASD often have with shifting their attention, and dealing with the difficulty of engaging students with ASD in activities for which they do not have interest or the skill set required. This does not mean that if you follow the lead of a student with ASD that the student will automatically begin interacting in a positive manner. The student may still try to escape from the interactions. If that happens, be sure to use additional strategies to establish interactions with the student. Do not just follow the student around; that is not the intention of this strategy. Follow the student's lead to increase the likelihood that the student will be able to engage, but then use a combination of other strategies to establish and maintain the interaction when necessary.

Behavioral Momentum

Behavioral momentum is a strategy that is used to increase a student's motivation to respond to tasks that are difficult or challenging. It involves making two or three requests that are easy for the student before making a request that is more difficult (Davis et al., 1994; Jung, Sainato, & Davis, 2008). Teachers can take note of what happens when a student with ASD is presented with challenging tasks one after the other. Typically, the student will shut down and stop trying because they do not feel they can be successful. If this is the case, using behavioral momentum can provide the motivation that these students need. For example, if a goal for the student is to identify vowel sounds, and the student already knows /a/ and /o/, the teacher can use the following teaching sequence:

1. Hold up an *a* for the student, and ask what sound it makes.

2. Hold up an *o* for the student, and ask what sound it makes.

3. Hold up an *i* for the student, and ask what sound it makes.

By making easy-easy-difficult requests, the student builds *momentum,* or confidence, and is more likely to attempt the challenging request. This pattern should be continued throughout the lesson or activity to maintain motivation.

Self-Monitoring

Self-monitoring is a strategy that involves teaching students how to monitor their own performance to increase motivation and promote positive behaviors. This strategy has been widely used to improve academics, social behaviors, and independent functioning of students with ASD (Coyle & Cole, 2004; Dipipi, Jitendra, & Miller, 2001; Koegel, Koegel, Hurley, & Frea, 1992; Pierce & Schreibman, 1994). When students are involved in recording their own behaviors, they become more aware of their own actions and may be more likely to improve their behaviors than if teachers are solely responsible for documenting performance. When using self-monitoring, Ganz (2008) suggested the following:

1. Select a specific goal or target behavior.

2. Discuss expectations with the student and provide a rationale for using self-monitoring.

3. Select a reinforcer.

4. Teach the student how to record performance and self-reinforce through role-play activities.

5. Both the teacher and the student initially record the student's performance, but teacher recording fades out once the student is consistently recording accurately.

Date		Student's name	
1/22		Jacob	
Name of assignment	I Finished the Assignment (Yes or No)	I Turned in the Assignment (Yes or No)	Points Earned (5 Points for Each Assignment Turned in)
Reading (Johnny Appleseed)	yes	yes	5
Math (multiplication sheet)	yes	yes	5
Writing (favorite animal)	no		
Centers (science activity)	yes	no	
			Total points earned: 10

Figure 5.1. Self-monitoring example for completing assignments.

Self-monitoring is particularly useful in general education classrooms because it lessens the amount of teacher involvement in managing behaviors, allowing the teacher to better meet the needs of all students in the classroom. Figure 5.1 provides an example of a self-monitoring tool for completing in-class assignments.

Prompting/Fading Procedure

Students with ASD often get "blamed" for being *prompt-dependent,* or reliant on certain cues or assistance in order to respond to certain requests or to make initiations. The truth is that if a student is prompt-dependent, teachers and parents are more to blame than the student. If adults do not systematically fade out the prompts they are giving to students, then students will certainly become reliant on those prompts. The prompting/fading procedure is a behavioral strategy that consists of teaching skills and behaviors by providing prompts or cues, but then fading out the intensity of the prompts as soon as possible to promote independent responding.

There are two different methods that can be used to fade prompts systematically: *least-to-most prompts* and *most-to-least prompts.* With least-to-most prompts, each time a request is made, the most minimal prompt possible is given to enable the student to respond successfully. However, if the student does not respond with the prompt provided, the teacher should increase the intensity of the response to enable the student to respond successfully. As requests are provided again and again, the most minimal prompt that the teacher thinks the student needs to display the desired behavior should be chosen. Eventually, the required prompt becomes less and less intensive, until no prompt is needed at all. For example, if you are teaching a student to answer comprehension questions during small-group reading, you may begin prompting the student by re-reading the section that entails the answer to the question if you think that is all the student needs to supply a correct response. If that prompt does not help the student to provide an answer, however, you need to increase the intensity of the prompt by showing the student the picture in the book related to the question. The next time you ask the student a question, the student should have an opportunity to respond without the picture cue. Whatever the prompt is that results in a successful student response, you should attempt to use a less-intensive prompt each time a new opportunity to respond is provided.

Using most-to-least prompts, you begin with intensive prompting to ensure success and then lessen the intensity of the initial prompts. For example, if you are teaching a student to line up with the class, at first you may take the student by the hand and walk the student to the line. Gradually, as future requests are made, the prompt can fade to walking next to the student without hand-holding, giving the direction face-to-face and then pointing to the line, giving the direction face-to-face without pointing to the line, giving the direction in close proximity to the student, and eventually giving the direction from anywhere in the room. Whether you are using most-to-least prompting or least-to-most prompting, you are still fading the intensity of the prompts as quickly as possible until the student can respond independently. The main difference is that with most-to-least-prompts, you begin with the most intensive prompt possible and fade it out, and with least-to-most prompts, you begin with the most minimal prompt you think the student may need to respond, increase the intensity of the prompts if necessary, and then fade them out.

How do you decide whether you should use least-to-most or most-to-least prompting? Generally, if the student does not have any of the skills required to respond to a certain request, most-to-least prompting is used to prevent frustration and task avoidance. However, if the student has some of the skills required, but not all, use least-to-most prompting to promote independent responding as quickly as possible and prevent prompt dependency.

There are several different types of prompts that can be used: physical, gestural, auditory, and visual (Wolery, Ault, & Doyle, 1992). Physical prompts entail some sort of touch. This can range from hand-over-hand assistance to a light tap to encourage a student to respond. Examples of verbal prompts include repeating directions, giving verbal reminders, or verbal redirection. Visual prompts may include objects, pictures, picture symbols, or written words. Gestural prompts may include pointing, nodding or shaking your head, holding up a certain number of fingers to refer to something, or using a gestural symbol, such as holding up a hand to indicate "stop." Some believe that physical prompts are the most intensive, followed by verbal, visual, and then gestural. However, this is not necessarily true. Consider teaching a student to complete seatwork independently. A physical prompt such as lightly touching the student's shoulder to encourage on-task behavior may actually be less intensive than a verbal prompt such as, "If you want to go to recess, you need to get your work done." Therefore, the type of prompt you are using is not necessarily what is most important. Whether you are systematically fading the intensity of prompts until the student does not require any prompts at all is what matters the most.

Embedded Discrete Trials

The *embedded discrete trials* strategy simply uses the teaching sequence presented by Lovaas (1987) within ongoing classroom routines and activities. The teaching sequence is as follows:

1. Antecedent (request, direction, comment, question, or other opportunity to respond)

2. Prompt (if necessary, but fade it out as soon as possible)

3. Behavior (student responds to the antecedent appropriately)

4. Consequence (positive reinforcement)

This teaching sequence can be used to teach many, many skills throughout the school day. For example, if one of the goals for a student is to respond to a comment made by the teacher, embedded discrete trials can be used during circle time, small-group instruction, whole-group instruction, centers, transitions, recess, and lunch. Below is an example of using an embedded discrete trial during centers to teach a student to respond to a comment.

Antecedent: The student is looking at a picture from a magazine, and the teacher joins the child in the writing center and says, "That is a funny picture."

Prompt: The student doesn't respond to the comment so the teacher says the comment again and points to something that is funny in the picture.

Behavior: The student says, "Frog."

Consequence: The teacher says, "Yes, the frog jumped on the dinner table!" and smiles at the student.

Modeling/Request Imitation

The *modeling/request imitation* strategy is another strategy that is not used often enough with students with ASD. The strategy entails first modeling or showing the student what you expect the student to do, then providing an opportunity for the student to imitate the model, with immediate support and feedback provided to the student (Buffington, Krantz, McClannahan, & Poulson, 1998). Some may consider this strategy to be one form of prompting; however, because teachers may provide intrusive prompts for students with ASD when they are not necessarily needed, this strategy gives teachers another approach to consider before helping the student too much. For example, if the goal is for the student to complete two-digit plus two-digit math problems with regrouping, the teacher can use modeling/request imitation by first demonstrating how to complete the problem, then giving the student a similar problem to complete. Although this sounds like common sense, teachers may jump right into giving verbal prompts such as, "Start in the ones column," "Put the one over the tens column," or "Don't forget to add the two."

If you use verbal prompts such as these too often, students can become dependent on them and will not be able to complete the problems independently. It is important to note that modeling/request imitation can and should be used multiple times while teaching a student to perform a certain skill or behavior. Teachers may model something during the initial teaching phase, but then refrain from modeling throughout the learning stages. Also, the request imitation part of the strategy is sometimes left out. Teachers use modeling quite naturally when teaching, but they do not always provide an opportunity for the student to imitate the model and give immediate support and feedback as the student attempts to imitate what was demonstrated.

Shaping

In behavioral language, the *shaping* strategy entails reinforcing successive approximations of a desired behavior (Cooper, Heron, & Heward, 1987). In other words, you use the shaping strategy by setting a desired outcome or goal and then positively reinforce the student as the student gets closer and closer to meeting the expectation. This requires teachers to understand that in order for a student with ASD to get from point A to point Z, the student must first go through B, C, D, and so forth. By reinforcing students as they make small improvements, they are more likely to be motivated to meet the next expectation. This is in contrast to providing negative consequences when students do not meet expectations. When students with ASD are not meeting teacher expectations, it is often because they lack the skills required, their anxiety gets in the way, or they lack motivation. Using the shaping procedure allows teachers to set small goals so that students can easily learn the required skills, which helps to reduce anxiety and increase motivation. A scenario that describes a teacher using shaping procedures to teach a student to raise his hand during whole-group instruction follows:

> Gabriel is a seventh-grade student who often shouts out answers to the teacher's questions during whole-group instruction. To teach Gabriel how to raise his hand and wait to be called on, his science teacher first began providing positive reinforcement to Gabriel when he raised his hand while he shouted out an answer. After providing specific academic praise, the teacher said "I'm glad you raised your hand. Next time please wait to be called on." The next time Gabriel raised his hand while shouting out, the teacher did not provide positive reinforcement. Instead the teacher reminded Gabriel to raise his hand and wait to be called on. When Gabriel then raised his hand without shouting out, the teacher called on him immediately and provided a positive comment about his response. The teacher then required Gabriel to wait a little longer each time before calling on him and providing specific academic praise for his answer. Eventually Gabriel was able to raise his hand and wait to be called on just like all of the other students in the class.

Contingent Imitation

Contingent imitation is somewhat similar to following the child's lead. This strategy entails imitating what the student is doing to establish an interaction (Cautilli &

Dziewolska, 2005; Gazdag & Warren, 2000). For example, if the student is building a tower with blocks, the teacher or a peer can get in close proximity to the student and imitate the student by building the same type of tower. Sometimes contingent imitation is the only way to get a student with ASD to attend to another individual if the student is deeply engaged in a certain activity. Once the student responds to the contingent imitation, however, attempt to then use modeling/request imitation to get the student to imitate the teacher or peer as well. Some may think it is inappropriate or strange to imitate a student with ASD if the student is engaging in stereotypic or self-stimulatory behavior. However, a situation in which an interventionist used contingent imitation when a student was engaging in self-stimulatory behavior to establish a successful positive interaction with a young child with ASD is as follows:

Amy, an early intervention specialist, was supporting a 4-year-old girl in a typical preschool classroom. One day Amy came into the classroom and approached the little girl. She asked the little girl for a hug, but the girl ignored her. She then asked the little girl for a high-five, but the girl ignored her. The problem was that the little girl was very engaged in tapping on the stars on the bulletin board in the classroom. It was a self-stimulatory behavior that consisted of tapping on one star with her knuckle then going on to the next star and the next and so on. So, after two failed attempts to get the little girl to acknowledge her, Amy decided to imitate the child by tapping on a star with her knuckle. Immediately, the little girl looked up at Amy and smiled. Amy then said, "Give me five," and the little girl did so. An interaction was established by first imitating the child's behavior and then quickly providing an opportunity for the child to respond to Amy.

Balanced Turn-Taking

Balanced turn-taking is a strategy that is useful in addressing a student's difficulty with social reciprocity. It entails the teacher or peer setting up a balanced, back-and-forth interaction to increase the length of attention and engagement of the student with ASD (Landa, 2007; MacDonald & Carroll, 1992; Noonan & McCormick, 2006). Although this may sound simple, it requires careful planning to set up activities and interactions that provide the support a student with ASD needs to maintain long chains of back-and-forth interactions. Teachers must consider the student's present level of performance to make sure the requests are developmentally appropriate for the student. The following scenario describes how balanced turn-taking was established between a student with ASD and a typically developing peer:

Brian, a fourth-grade student with autism, mastered his basic multiplication facts. His teacher used this strength to set up an activity for Brian and a peer that would encourage balanced turn-taking. The students were given one set of multiplication flash cards. They were instructed to split the deck of cards in half and take turns presenting a card to one another to answer aloud. This activity enabled Brian to maintain long chains of back-and-forth interactions with a peer because it was structured, and he had already mastered the multiplication skills needed to respond appropriately.

Task Analysis

In Chapter 3, *task analysis* was discussed as a method for assessing independent functioning skills. It can also be used as an effective teaching strategy for students with ASD. The task analysis strategy involves breaking an individual task down into sequential steps that can then be taught to the student in a stepwise fashion. There are three ways to use task analysis: forward chaining, backward chaining, and whole-task presentation. *Forward chaining* involves teaching the first step, then the second, then the third, and so forth until the student can complete the entire task independently. *Backward chaining* involves teaching the last step, the second-to-last step, and so forth until the student can complete the entire task independently. *Whole-task presentation* involves gradually increasing the student's participation by involving the student in more and more steps of the task with each new opportunity, but not necessarily starting with the first or last step. Instead the student is involved in the steps that are the easiest for the student to do first. Whether you use forward chaining, backward chaining, or whole-task presentation depends on the task being taught and the individual student. For example, you may use forward chaining to teach a student how to turn on the computer because each step of the task is at the same level of difficulty for the student. However, you may use backward chaining to teach a student to wash hands because the easiest part is throwing the paper towel in the garbage. You may use whole-task presentation to teach a student to compute long division problems because there are skills in the middle of the task that the student has already mastered. Task analysis can be used to teach daily living skills, positive behaviors, social skills, communication skills, and academic skills. An example of a task analysis for a vocabulary activity at the language arts center follows:

1.   Choose a picture from the basket.

2.   Glue the picture on your paper.

3.   Write a definition of the item in the picture using your own words.

4.   Write a sentence that includes the item in the picture.

The teacher would probably choose to use forward chaining to teach a student how to complete this task because the steps increase in difficulty.

Video Modeling

Video modeling is a strategy used to teach students with ASD to imitate certain behaviors by watching a video model of another student engaging in the desired behavior (Bellini, Akullian, & Hopf, 2007). Teachers can also use video self-modeling that involves showing students videos of themselves engaging in a desired behavior to increase the use of that specific behavior (Dowrick, 1999). Digital cameras that have video capability are quite useful for implementing this strategy because teachers can quickly capture a behavior on video and upload it to the computer for students to view. This strategy can be quite useful when including students with ASD in general education classrooms because there are many positive models to capture on video demonstrating the behaviors teachers want the students to learn. Once the behaviors are caught on video, the students can view them, talk about what they observed, role-play what they observed, and then be reinforced for demonstrating those behaviors in the natural context of the classroom. A variety of positive behaviors and social, communication, academic, and independent functioning skills can be taught through video modeling or video self-modeling, such as lining up, interactive play skills, on-task behavior, greeting others, asking for help, and turning in assignments.

Social Stories

Social Stories (Gray & Garand, 1993) have been used with students with ASD to teach a variety of social skills and positive behaviors. The strategy entails writing a short story that clearly illustrates behavioral expectations. They are usually written from a student's perspective to allow the student to relate to the information provided in the story. The following is an example of a Social Story used to teach a student with ASD in the general education classroom how to ask for help:

> My name is James, and I am in fourth grade. I am a smart student who tries very hard with my schoolwork. Sometimes I get stuck on something and need help from my teacher. That is okay. Many students need help from the teacher. When I need help, I raise my hand quietly and wait for the teacher to come over. When the teacher comes over, I ask for help. My teacher likes when I ask for help when I need it, so I can learn.

Social Stories can be used in conjunction with a variety of other strategies to increase their benefit. Teachers can ask students comprehension questions about the stories and engage them in role plays to increase their effectiveness (Chan & O'Reilly, 2008). Video modeling can also be used with Social Stories to enhance learning (Sansosti & Powell-Smith, 2008). It is quite easy to use PowerPoint to create the Social Story and insert pictures of the student and videos of the student or other students demonstrating the expectations. The use of prompting/fading procedures and positive reinforcement are also effective when teaching students the behaviors targeted in the Social Stories (Swaggart et al., 1995). Students can also be taught to use self-monitoring strategies to record their own performance related to meeting the expectations set forth in the Social Stories (Thiemann & Goldstein, 2001).

Peer-Mediated Intervention

Peer-mediated intervention is a strategy that utilizes typically developing peers to create meaningful learning opportunities for students with ASD. Peers are trained to use behavioral strategies such as the ones discussed in this chapter to promote positive interactions with students with ASD (Morrison, Kamps, Garcia, & Parker, 2001). Without training and support provided to typically developing peers, they often refrain from interacting with students with ASD because the students may not respond to their initiations (DiSalvo & Oswald, 2002). However, when peers learn how to get a student with ASD to respond, they are often positively reinforced by the response and increase their initiations with the student without the need for many teacher reminders to do so (Robertson, Green, Alper, Schloss, & Kohler, 2003). Teachers can use peer-mediated interventions to improve social interaction skills, increase participation in academic activities, and promote positive behaviors.

Direct Instruction

Direct instruction is an explicit teaching model that has been shown to be effective for decades (Breen, Haring, Pitts-Conway, & Gaylord-Ross, 1985; Haring & Ryndak, 1994). Although there are specific direct instruction curriculum materials, such as *Reading Mastery* (McGraw-Hill, 2008), *Language for Learning* (McGraw-Hill, 1999), and *Distar Arithmetic* (McGraw-Hill, 1992), the direct instruction teaching model can be used to teach just about any skill. The model consists of five steps:

1. Introduction (rationale, access background knowledge, motivate the learner)

2. Lesson presentation (provide a short mini-lesson to teach the specific skill)

3. Guided practice (provide opportunities for the students to demonstrate the skill with teacher support)

4. Independent practice (students demonstrate the skill without teacher support and receive immediate feedback)

5. Closure/generalization (summarize what was learned; provide opportunities for students to use the skill across a variety of contexts with feedback provided)

Teachers can use this teaching model to teach academic skills, behavioral expectations, social skills, communication skills, and independent functioning skills. This can be used as a whole-group lesson, small-group lesson, or one-to-one instruction.

Designing Technological Teaching Procedures

The behavioral strategies discussed in this chapter can be used in conjunction with one another to develop technological teaching procedures for specific goals for students with ASD. Some teaching procedures may only include one of the strategies

Table 5.3. Behavioral teaching strategies

Strategy	Brief explanation
Positive reinforcement	After a student demonstrates a desired behavior, provide a consequence that is rewarding to increase the likelihood that the behavior will occur again in the future.
Time delay	Provide a brief period of wait time paired with an expectant look and expectant body language to encourage the student to initiate or respond.
Environmental arrangements	Place desired items out of reach, give small amounts of a desired item, do something unexpected, or adjust environmental stimuli.
Following the child's lead	Attend to what the student is attending to for purposes of establishing a positive interaction.
Behavioral momentum	Use a pattern of easy-easy-difficult requests to enhance student motivation.
Self-monitoring	Teach students how to monitor their own performance using self-assessment tools.
Prompting/fading procedure	Provide assistance to enable the student to respond successfully, then systematically fade out the assistance provided until the student can meet the expectation independently.
Embedded discrete trials	Provide an antecedent (opportunity for the student to respond or initiate), prompt if necessary, and provide positive reinforcement after the student responds appropriately.
Modeling/request imitation	Demonstrate what the student is expected to do, provide an opportunity for the student to imitate, and provide feedback and support when the student imitates the model or attempts to imitate the model.
Shaping	Reinforce successive approximations of a desired behavior to get the student closer and closer to the end goal.
Contingent imitation	Imitate what the student is doing for purposes of establishing a positive interaction.
Balanced turn-taking	Structure interactions with the student to establish long chains of back-and-forth interactions.
Task analysis	Break down a task into individual steps and teach them using forward chaining, backward chaining, or whole-task presentation.
Video modeling/video self-modeling	Show the student video clips of peers or the actual student demonstrating a desired behavior to increase the student's use of the behavior shown in the video.
Social Stories	Write short stories written from the student's perspective using clear statements that teach behavioral or social expectations.
Peer-mediated intervention	Teach peers strategies for promoting positive interactions between peers and the student.
Direct instruction	Provide explicit instruction, including an introduction, lesson presentation, guided practice, independent practice, and closure/generalization.

discussed, whereas others may include a variety of the strategies within one teaching procedure. Table 5.3 provides a list of the strategies discussed in this chapter, with a short explanation for each one for teachers to use as a reminder when developing teaching procedures. Although it is true that behavioral strategies must be included in the teaching procedures for the interventions to be considered ABA, this does not mean that other evidence-based teaching practices cannot or should not be included as well when appropriate. For example, when developing teaching procedures for teaching a student how to answer comprehension questions, you may include behavioral strategies such as embedded discrete trials and time delay, but you may also suggest having the student listen to books on tape before reading material independently to improve comprehension.

When writing teaching procedures, it is recommended that you include the actual behavioral strategies in bold, but also provide specific examples. This increases the consistency of implementation. The more clear and specific the teaching procedures are, the more likely different individuals will be able to implement them in the same manner. Also, to address generality (one of the ABA dimensions), it is best to write the teaching procedures so they can be implemented across a variety of contexts and settings. Table 5.4 includes an example of technological teaching procedures that use behavioral strategies to teach a student how to respond to comments. Notice that these teaching procedures can easily be implemented in any setting with different peers and adults. Chapter 7 includes many sample ABA teaching plans that include technological, conceptual procedures written in such a way that students can generalize the skills they are learning.

Table 5.4. Example of technological teaching procedures

Goal

The student will independently respond to comments related to current activity.

Teaching procedures

1. When the student is engaged in an activity, make a comment about what the student is doing.
2. If the student responds, provide *positive reinforcement* by making an additional positive comment or specific praise, smiling, or joining the child in the activity if that would be enjoyable to the student.
3. If the student doesn't respond to the comment, use *time delay* to encourage the student to respond. For example, while drawing, you might say, "I like your picture," and wait with an expectant look. If the child responds, provide positive reinforcement. For example, if the student then says, "I'm drawing a sun," you might smile and say, "Your sun looks beautiful!"
4. If the student doesn't respond given the time delay, try stating the comment again or rephrasing the comment in a way you think the student may respond. If still no response, use *embedded discrete trials* to ensure a response. For example, state the comment again, and if the child doesn't respond, provide a prompt. The prompt may include a fill-in so the child can respond to the comment. For example, you may say, "I'm drawing a _____," to encourage the student to fill in the sentence to respond to the comment, "I like your picture." You can also use a gestural prompt, such as pointing to the picture of the sun after making the comment, to encourage the student to respond. Once the student responds, provide positive reinforcement. Be sure to fade out the types of prompts you provide as you provide additional embedded discrete trials for more learning opportunities. Although you can ask the student a question as a prompt, such as "What are you drawing?", that should be a last resort. The reason is that many students learn to answer questions but not comments. If we prompt a student to respond to a comment by asking a question, we are actually teaching the student to respond to a question once again. However, if you do need to ask a question to get a response, follow up immediately with the original comment to encourage the child to respond without the question prompt.

Chapter Summary

The strategies presented in this chapter represent a sample of behavioral strategies that can be used to teach social interaction, communication, academic, behavioral, and independent functioning skills. When developing ABA teaching procedures, you are likely to use many of the strategies in conjunction with one another, as was done in the example provided in Table 5.4. The strategies were organized according to whether they are used to increase skill performance or skill acquisition. However, this does not mean that you cannot use some of the skill performance strategies if you are developing teaching procedures for a skill a student is acquiring. In fact, positive reinforcement should be included in all teaching procedures, whether the focus is skill performance or skill acquisition. The most important aspect of developing ABA teaching procedures is that the procedures are conceptual and technological. The procedures should include behavioral strategies such as the ones included in this chapter, and they should be written in a detailed, specific manner to ensure that all teachers implement the interventions in the same manner.

6

Data Collection and Analysis

· ·

Teachers often moan and groan when the phrases *data collection* and *progress monitoring* come up. They often think, "I just want to be able to teach and not worry about collecting data." The truth is, data collection is the only way to really know that your students are learning what you are teaching them. This negative perception of data collection is likely tied to the fact that most teachers are not properly trained to use a variety of different meaningful and practical data collection methods. Data collection can actually be quite reinforcing for teachers when used consistently, because they are able to truly see the progress their students are making day to day. This chapter includes a rationale for data collection, a description of a variety of different data collection methods, sample data sheets, and procedures for determining mastery and responding when students are not making progress.

Rationale for Data Collection

Those familiar with ABA teaching procedures know that data collection is essential. However, the rationale for data collection is not always completely understood. In many situations where ABA teaching is being implemented, the students receive one-to-one instruction in special education settings. The teachers often have "the book" for each student receiving ABA. The book typically includes tons of data sheets and is quite large. What some fail to understand is that data collection is not about collecting a pile of data sheets to prove that data is being collected. In fact, there is no point in taking data if the information is not graphed and analyzed regularly to make instructional decisions. There are two main purposes for data collection: to monitor progress and to determine mastery. Using data collection to monitor progress means that teachers examine the data regularly to determine whether the student is making adequate gains or not. Using data collection to determine mastery means that teachers use the data to know when the student has met the specific objective. When goals are initially written, they must include criteria for mastery, as was discussed in Chapter 4. The criteria for mastery typically indicate the methods for data collection. For example, if the criterion for mastery is 80% accuracy, percentage data should be collected. When implementing ABA teaching procedures in general education classrooms, the methods of collecting data have to be appropriate and feasible considering the context of the classroom. There is a big difference between data collection methods that general education teachers are likely to use and methods that self-contained special education teachers use. Thus the section that follows provides descriptions of a variety of data collection methods that are user-friendly in the general education classroom.

Data Collection Procedures

Whatever data collection method you use, it is important to graph the data to allow for visual analysis. A collection of numbers and data sheets does not allow for easy interpretations of the data. When data are presented visually, you can clearly see student progress or lack thereof. This allows you to make instructional decisions early on to ensure students make adequate gains throughout the school year. When you meet with parents for conferences or IEP meetings, having visual representation of the data helps them to understand the progress their child is making. This is also helpful for other IEP team members. Graphing data does not need to be time-consuming. In fact, every data collection method discussed in this chapter can be adapted into a basic graph in a matter of seconds.

It is important to collect data on a regular basis. You cannot decide to take data whenever it is convenient or whenever you happen to remember. For some objectives, daily data collection is most appropriate. For others, taking data three times a week is sufficient. Even data collection once a week for certain goals may be all that is needed. However, it is necessary to continue to take data consistently and use the same frequency of data collection week after week. Otherwise, your data may be skewed. For example, if a teacher randomly takes data, it may be that data is collected only when the student performs poorly or only when the student performs extremely well. In general, it is always best to take data daily if that is possible given the context of the classroom and the nature of the objectives. Frequent data collection is much easier when you have a variety of different procedures to select from. Percentage data, level of independence data, individualized rating systems, frequency data, and yes/no data are discussed in detail next.

Percentage Data

The most common data collection method for monitoring progress and determining mastery for IEP objectives and goals for ABA interventions is *percentage data*. Considering the context of the general education classroom, percentage data collection is usually appropriate for many academic goals. For example, progress on goals related to reading comprehension, mathematics, spelling, and content area instruction can often be monitored with percentage data simply by using work samples. If a student completes 10 math problems, answers 5 comprehension questions, spells 10 words on a spelling test, or takes an end-of-unit multiple choice test in social studies or science, it is quite easy to get a percentage correct by dividing the number correct by the total number of problems or questions. Percentage data can also be used for task completion very easily by dividing the number of assignments a student turned in by the number of assignments given during a particular day or week.

Percentage data collection is often overused, however, and is not always the most appropriate method for collecting data, depending on the goals of the students. For example, progress on many communication and social interaction goals is not so easily monitored using percentage data. Consider the following goal: "Jessica will request desired items using simple sentences with 80% accuracy." Goals like this are common in IEPs for students with ASD, but the reality is that teachers do not always know how many opportunities a student has in a given period of time to request desired items because they cannot get into the brains of the students to know when they actually want or need something. If the number of opportunities is unknown, percentage data collection is not possible. Consider this goal: "David will engage in joint play with peers during recess 70% of the time." If teachers were monitoring progress for this goal using percentage data, that would mean they would need to count how many minutes David engages in joint play during recess and divide that by the total number of minutes the students are at recess. This is not a realistic data collection method for general education teachers when they are responsible for the rest of the class during recess as well. Although percentage data collection is useful for some objectives, it is important for teachers to understand that it is not always the most appropriate method.

A sample percentage data collection sheet is shown in Figure 6.1. This data sheet is designed so that teachers can either simply circle the percentage correct for the particular date or take *trial-by-trial data*. Taking trial-by-trial data means that each

Student's name						Objective				
Jessica						Inferential comprehension questions				
Trials	Date 9/03		Date 9/04		Date 9/05		Date		Date	
10	C/I	100%	C/I	100%	C/I	100%	C/I	100%	C/I	100%
9	C/I	90%	C/I	90%	C/I	90%	C/I	90%	C/I	90%
8	C/I	80%	C/I	80%	C/I	(80%)	C/I	80%	C/I	80%
7	C/I	70%	C/I	70%	C/I	70%	C/I	70%	C/I	70%
6	C/I	60%	C/I	60%	C/I	60%	C/I	60%	C/I	60%
5	C/I	50%	C/I	(50%)	C/I	50%	C/I	50%	C/I	50%
4	C/I	(40%)	C/I	40%	C/I	40%	C/I	40%	C/I	40%
3	C/I	30%	C/I	30%	C/I	30%	C/I	30%	C/I	30%
2	C/I	20%	C/I	20%	C/I	20%	C/I	20%	C/I	20%
1	C/I	10%	C/I	10%	C/I	10%	C/I	10%	C/I	10%

Figure 6.1. Percentage correct data sheet. (*Key:* C, correct; I, incorrect.)

time there is an opportunity for a student to respond, the teacher will circle either *c* for correct or *i* for incorrect. Incorrect should also be used if the student does not respond at all or requires prompting to respond. Then the percentage correct is determined by dividing the number of correct responses by the total number of opportunities. To create a visual representation of the data, circle the percentage and draw a line to connect the previous date's score to the current score. Teachers can use their own percentage data sheets or use computer programs, such as Excel, to record and graph percentage data. Remember: data are collected and visually displayed so that progress can be monitored to allow teachers to make informed instructional decisions and to determine when mastery has been achieved.

Level of Independence Data

Level of independence data collection is simple and informative and can be used to monitor progress and document mastery for many goals and objectives. This method is used by creating a rating system that indicates how much support the student needs to meet the objective. An example of a rating system that can be used for taking level of independence data follows:

1. Maximum prompting (the student requires extensive amounts of assistance and is not showing any independence)

2. Moderate prompting (the student requires assistance but shows some independence)

3. Minimal prompting (the student is almost independent but requires a small amount of assistance)

4. Independent (the student performs the skill without any assistance)

When using a rating system such as this, the teacher records the student's average performance for a given period of time. The period of time can be a whole school day, partial school day, or class period. With this data collection system, trial-by-trial data collection is not necessary. The teacher simply records how much assistance the student required overall. For example, if the student requires maximum prompting most of the day, but there were a couple of opportunities in which the student performed with moderate levels of assistance, the teacher should still indicate maximum prompting for that day. A good rule of thumb is that if you are unsure which number to record, record the lower number. This is not to suggest that you are setting low expectations for your students. It is just best to err on the low side so as not to cut off intervention prematurely. If a teacher inaccurately gauges a student as independent, that data could make teachers overlook or remove important supports that the student needs. Another option is to record 1.5, 2.5, or 3.5 if the student is between two ratings.

   If more than one person is collecting data on a specific objective, it is important to discuss examples of student performance for each rating to ensure progress is being recorded reliably. Consider the following objective: "Grant will independently raise

Objective	
Grant will independently raise his hand, wait to be called on, and ask for teacher assistance when he needs help with an assignment.	
Rating	**Example**
1: Maximum prompting	The teacher approaches Grant when he is showing signs of frustration and physically assists him to raise his hand and/or provides him with the words to use to ask for help.
2: Moderate prompting	The teacher approaches Grant when he is showing signs of frustration and points to a cue card that shows a student raising his hand to ask for help. When Grant raises his hand, the teacher says something such as, "Ask me for help if you need assistance."
3: Minimal prompting	Before Grant begins work, the teacher reminds him to raise his hand and ask for assistance if he needs help. A visual cue card is left on his desk as a reminder.
4: Independent	When Grant needs assistance during a variety of different tasks, he raises his hand, waits to be called on, and asks for help without any prompting to do so.

Figure 6.2. Level of independence example.

his hand, wait to be called on, and ask for teacher assistance when he needs help with an assignment." First notice that the word *independently* is used in the objective to indicate the criteria for mastery. You can also add a statement such as "across different subject areas" to make the criteria for mastery more specific. If Grant is in middle or high school and has several different teachers, all teachers need to be on the same page when it comes to recording his level of independence for this objective. Figure 6.2 shows an example of each rating for Grant's level of independence with raising his hand to ask for assistance. This type of description for each level of independence rating is often helpful to ensure that data are collected in a meaningful way. Without giving specific performance examples, teachers may not record data accurately. With specific examples, teachers can record the rating with much more confidence, because the type of assistance provided is listed for each rating.

Figure 6.3 shows an example of a data collection sheet for level of independence data. This sheet allows teachers to collect data for several objectives using a level of independence rating system. If the teacher is collecting data on a student's performance across the school day, at the end of the day the teacher can create a graphical display of the data simply by circling the level of independence rating for each objective and drawing a line to connect to the previous day's rating. It literally may take only 10 seconds for the teacher to record a student's level of independence data each day, depending on how many objectives the student has.

Student's name				Michael			
Objective	Date 10/15	Date 10/16	Date 10/17	Date 10/18	Date 10/19	Date 10/22	Date 10/23
Yes/no questions	4 3 2 ①─	4 3 2 ─①	4 3 ② 1	4 3 ② 1	4 3 ② 1	4 ③── 2 1	4 ──③ 2 1
	Date	Date	Date	Date	Date	Date	Date
Initiating greetings	4 3 2 ①─	4 3 ② 1	4 3 ② 1	4 3 ② 1	4 3 ② 1	4 ③ 2 1	4 3 ② 1

Figure 6.3. Level of independence data sheet. (1 = Maximum prompting; 2 = Moderate prompting; 3 = Minimal prompting; 4 = Independent.)

Individualized Rating System

Teachers can also develop an *individualized rating system* if the level of independence rating system is not appropriate or meaningful. The same data collection sheet can be used as is used for level of independence, but the numbers can represent something else. Consider this objective: "Marla will imitate all consonant and vowel sounds to provide the initial sound for items she wants or sees." Notice that the word *all* is used to indicate the criteria for mastery. An individualized rating system such as the one that follows can be used to measure progress toward this goal:

1. Marla does not imitate any consonant or vowel sounds.

2. Marla imitates very few consonant and vowel sounds.

3. Marla imitates many consonant and vowel sounds.

4. Marla imitates most consonant and vowel sounds.

5. Marla imitates all consonant and vowel sounds.

Of course, the data collection sheet should include numbers 1 through 5 instead of 1 through 4 if you are using a rating system such as the preceding one. Although it is generally easier to stick with a generic level of independence rating system, there will be some objectives that require something more original to measure progress. For example, the objective "Alex will respond to comments from peers and adults across a variety of instructional and noninstructional activities" would probably be best monitored using an individualized rating system that includes number ranges such as

0: Does not respond to any comments

1: Responds to comments from adults only

2: Responds to comments from adults and peers during very few activities

3: Responds to comments from adults and peers during most activities

4: Responds to comments from adults and peers during all activities

The objective "Christy will engage in reciprocal conversations with peers during academic and nonacademic activities with at least three back-and-forth exchanges each time" would also lend itself to the use of an individualized rating system such as

0: Usually no back-and-forth exchanges

1: Usually one back-and-forth exchange

2: Usually two back-and-forth exchanges

3: Usually three back-and-forth exchanges

Frequency Data

There are some objectives for which *frequency data collection* will be most appropriate. This entails recording the number of times something occurs. Consider the following objective: "Brian will raise his hand to answer questions at least five times during each whole-group instructional lesson." It would be easier for the teacher to record the number of times Brian raises his hand during each whole-group instructional lesson than to try to figure out some sort of percentage. If the criteria for mastery indicates a number, usually frequency data collection is the best way to monitor progress toward meeting the goal. Figure 6.4 provides a sample frequency data collection sheet. The teacher can use this by putting a slash next to a number each time the student displays the specific behavior. For example, when Brian raises his hand the first time, the teacher will put a slash next to the number 1. Each time Brian raises his hand after that, the teacher can put a slash next to the next number. After the lesson, the teacher can circle the total number of times Brian raised his hand. The total number for each column should be connected with a line to create a graphical display of the data for purposes of monitoring progress and determining mastery. In this scenario, the teacher may provide more than one whole-group instructional lesson each day. This does not mean that data need to be taken each time. The teacher can pick one lesson each day and just indicate the subject area to ensure Brian is learning to raise his hand across subjects. In fact, there is no rule that data need to be collected daily. Data can be collected every other day, every third day, or even once a week, depending on the objective.

Student's name			Objective			
Brian			Raise hand to answer questions at least five times during whole-group instruction.			
	Date 5/01	Date 5/02	Date 5/03	Date 5/04	Date	Date
Total number of hand raises	10	10	10	10	10	10
	9	9	9	9	9	9
	8	8	8	8	8	8
	7	7	7	7	7	7
	6	6	6	6	6	6
	5	5	5	5	5	5
	4	4	⟋ 4	4	4	4
	⟋ 3	3	⟋ 3	⟋ 3	3	3
	⟋ 2	2	⟋ 2	⟋ 2	2	2
	⟋ 1	⟋ 1	⟋ 1	⟋ 1	1	1
	0	0	0	0	0	0

Figure 6.4. Frequency data sheet.

Yes/No Data

Some objectives will simply require the teacher to record *yes/no data,* or whether or not the specific behavior was demonstrated. Consider the following objective: "Without prompting, Jamie will greet at least one peer upon entering the classroom each morning." For this objective, the teacher would only need to indicate *yes* if Jamie greeted a peer or *no* if Jamie did not greet a peer or needed prompting to do so. Figure 6.5 shows an example of a data collection sheet that can be used when taking yes/no data. The teacher simply circles *y* or *n* and draws a line to connect the previous date to the current date to create a graphical representation of the data.

Selecting a Data Collection Procedure

There is no set rule for which type of data collection procedure should be used for each objective written for a student. However, there are some things that teachers can consider when deciding how to collect data. The first thing to consider is how the criteria for mastery are stated. If the criteria for mastery indicate a percentage, then percentage data collection should be used. If the criteria indicate that the student will demonstrate

Student's name					Jamie				
Objective	Date 3/01	Date 3/02	Date 3/03	Date 3/04	Date 3/05	Date 3/08	Date 3/09	Date	Date
Greet at least one peer when entering the class each morning	Y	Y	Y	X	Y	Y	Y	Y	Y
	N	N	N	N	N	N	N	N	N
Remain in seat in the cafeteria for 10 minutes	Y	Y	Y	Y	Y	Y	Y	Y	Y
	N	N	N	N	N	N	N	N	N
	Y	Y	Y	Y	Y	Y	Y	Y	Y
	N	N	N	N	N	N	N	N	N
	Y	Y	Y	Y	Y	Y	Y	Y	Y
	N	N	N	N	N	N	N	N	N
	Y	Y	Y	Y	Y	Y	Y	Y	Y
	N	N	N	N	N	N	N	N	N
	Y	Y	Y	Y	Y	Y	Y	Y	Y
	N	N	N	N	N	N	N	N	N

Figure 6.5. Yes/no data collection sheet.

the skill independently (or without prompting), then level of independence data should be used. If the criteria include a specific behavioral expectation, then an individualized rating system may be appropriate. If the criteria indicate that the behavior should be displayed a specific number of times during a given time period, then frequency data can be taken. If the criteria indicate that the behavior should happen once each day or once each time period, then yes/no data can be collected.

Another thing to consider when selecting a data collection procedure is ease of use. If the general education teacher is the one responsible for data collection, the methods of collecting data must be feasible considering the responsibilities the teacher has during the school day. Level of independence data collection is probably the easiest and quickest way for general education teachers to collect meaningful data. It does take time initially to determine what each level of independence rating means for each specific objective, but after that, it is just a matter of circling a number at the end of the school day for each objective. Percentage data collection is easy for general education teachers when they already have the work samples to use to determine the percentage correct or percentage of assignments turned in. They are usually quite familiar with using percentage data for summative assessments such as quizzes and tests. The only difference is that when taking percentage data for ABA intervention, the data are more formative in nature in that they are used to make ongoing instructional decisions, and they are taken throughout the week as opposed to at the end of the week or the end of a unit.

One last thing to consider when selecting a data collection procedure is how you plan to teach the skill. For example, if you plan to teach the skill by using prompting/fading procedures, then using level of independence data collection makes perfect sense because you are simply recording how much prompting was needed. If you plan to teach something using a task analysis, you can record percentage data by taking the number of steps the student completed independently and dividing that by the total number of steps to get a percentage.

Determining Mastery

Chapter 4 discussed writing objectives to include a criterion for mastery. Collecting data allows teachers to determine when mastery has been achieved. Again, there is no rule for how long a student should display a certain skill for it to be considered mastered. It may depend on how often data are being collected. If data are collected daily, it may be best to have at least 5 consecutive days of data at the mastery level before indicating the objective is mastered. Many times students will achieve mastery Wednesday, Thursday, and Friday because they had Monday and Tuesday to learn a specific skill, but when they come back to school after the weekend, they are no longer at the mastery level. If the data collection procedures are fairly easy, go ahead and take data for 2 weeks to make sure the student has truly mastered the skill. On the other hand, if data are not being collected daily, having 5 consecutive days to determine mastery would not be appropriate. If data are collected three times a week, mastery can be determined when the student is performing the skill independently for three consecutive data points. If data are being collected weekly, it may be most appropriate to indicate mastery when the student performs the desired skill for 4 consecutive weeks. Thus there is no set rule for determining when mastery will be indicated. It is up to the team to decide what is most appropriate. However, be sure that you are not indicating mastery too early because the student may not have fully learned what was expected and may still require explicit instruction and progress monitoring.

Responding to Lack of Progress

Remember, one of the dimensions of ABA is that the interventions must be effective (see Chapter 2). In other words, if the student is not progressing, changes must be made. Also remember that the main purpose of data collection is to monitor progress.

When doing so, you examine the data to make instructional decisions. If progress is not being made, something must be done to address the problem. Many teachers first assume that the teaching procedures should be changed if the student is not making progress, but before making that assumption, teachers should consider the following hierarchy of questions:

1. Have the procedures been implemented correctly?

2. Have data been collected properly?

3. Do the teaching procedures need to be changed or altered?

4. Does the goal need to be changed or altered?

Procedures for implementing ABA interventions should be technological, which means that there are written procedures that should be followed when teaching the specific skill. If progress is not being made, it is important to first ask whether the procedures are actually being implemented as planned. If the answer is no, the general education teacher may need some support from the special education teacher to learn how to implement the teaching procedures. If it is determined that the teaching procedures are being implemented correctly, then determine whether data are being collected properly. Sometimes it may appear as if progress is not being made, but in fact the teacher is simply not collecting data in a consistent or correct manner. Also, sometimes the data collection method may need to be changed. For example, if percentage data is being used and the student is scoring 0% consistently and is seemingly not making progress, it may be helpful to change to level of independence data collection to be able to show whether or not the student is learning to be more independent and require less assistance from the teacher. If data collection is correct, consistent, and meaningful, then it would be appropriate to consider whether or not the teaching procedures should be changed or altered. There is no one set way to teach any skill, so if something is not working, design a different set of teaching procedures. However, remember that the teaching procedures must still be conceptual and utilize principles of behavior. If after changing the teaching procedures progress is still not being made, it may be appropriate to consider changing or altering the goal. It may be that the goal is not developmentally appropriate for that student, and there is a prerequisite skill that must be taught first.

Chapter Summary

Data collection and analysis should help teachers improve their instruction and not be seen as "just one more thing to do." By using the data collection and analysis methods discussed in this chapter, teachers can easily document and monitor student progress to make meaningful instructional decisions. Collecting and interpreting data enables teachers to enhance their quality of instruction and truly know when students have mastered specific skills.

7

Putting It All Together

• •

Now it's time to take everything discussed in this book and show how it all gets put together. This chapter provides a format for developing ABA teaching plans and includes five sample plans. Suggestions are provided for clarifying the roles individual team members will play when implementing ABA interventions in general education classrooms.

Format for Developing ABA Teaching Plans

It can be quite overwhelming to create ABA teaching plans for your students. Having a template to follow can make the process easier. After conducting and interpreting assessments and selecting goals and objectives as discussed in Chapters 3 and 4, you can use a format such as the sample provided in Appendix F to design your ABA teaching plans. This format includes a place to write the student's name, objective, data collection procedures, and teaching procedures. Notice there is a box next to the data collection options. In that section, you can provide a specific explanation for how data will be collected. For example, if a level of independence rating or individualized rating system is used, that section can include specific examples for each rating. If percentage data is used, specific explanations can be included for how the percentage is to be calculated. The teaching procedures are numbered to help the teachers implement the interventions in a stepwise fashion. Although the sample provided has space for up to 10 steps, most teaching procedures will have fewer steps.

Sample ABA Teaching Plans

It is easiest to begin using ABA interventions in your own classroom by getting an idea of how others have used such interventions. The sample ABA teaching plans included in Figures 7.1–7.5 can serve as models for writing plans for your own students.

Student	Objective
Gregory	Accurately respond to at least 5 literal comprehension questions during read-aloud activities for 5 consecutive school days.

Data Collection Procedures:

❏ Percentage Data

❏ Level of Independence Data

❏ Individualized Rating System

☑ Frequency Data

❏ Yes/No Data

> **Explanation of Data Collection Procedures:**
>
> Record and graph the number of correct responses without prompts during each read-aloud activity.

Teaching Procedures:

Use these **embedded discrete trial** procedures during small-group, whole-group, or one-to-one reading activities:

1. Read a small section of the material aloud to the students. This may be a few sentences, one page from a book, or a few pages from a book, depending on Gregory's ability to retain information read aloud.

2. Ask a literal comprehension question to the group. If Gregory raises his hand, call on him and move on to Step 3. If Gregory does not raise his hand, call his name to get his attention and repeat the question.

3. Do not say, "no" if Gregory answers incorrectly. Instead, restate or rephrase the question to see if he can self-correct. If he still cannot answer correctly, provide **least-to-most prompts.** For example, if the question was, "What did the family eat at the picnic?" you can prompt him by providing a fill-in such as "The family ate _____." If Gregory cannot respond, you can have him look at the picture to answer the question. If necessary, point to the picture of the food items to prompt him to answer the question. If a great deal of prompting is necessary for Gregory to respond, restate the question after he comes up with the correct answer to attempt to have him respond to the question directly without the prompting.

4. Provide **positive reinforcement** for all attempts to answer the question.

5. Use **shaping** procedures by gradually increasing the amount of material you read aloud before asking a question and following Steps 3 and 4 to enhance Gregory's ability to listen and comprehend for longer and longer periods of time.

Note: Although you cannot call on Gregory each time a question is asked or each time he raises his hand due to the needs of the other students, call on him as often as possible until he is able to engage independently and successfully during these comprehension activities.

Figure 7.1. Sample ABA teaching plan: academic.

The sample teaching plans provide one example each for academics, behavior, social interaction, communication, and independent functioning. See Appendixes A–E for additional examples for each of the five domains.

The plans included are a sampling of some common objectives that require explicit ABA instruction for students with ASD in general education classrooms. These plans would most likely need to be adapted for specific students to address individual needs and relate to the context of their classrooms, but they do provide a framework and a starting place. Notice that the behavioral strategies indicated in the teaching procedures are in bold. This is recommended to ensure that the teaching procedures are, in fact, conceptual (Chapter 2). Positive reinforcement is used in every teaching plan. Refer back to Chapter 5 for a variety of ways that positive reinforcement can be

Student	Objective
Craig	Independently follow one-step directions given to the whole class by the classroom teacher.

Data Collection Procedures:

❏ Percentage Data

☑ Level of Independence Data

❏ Individualized Rating System

❏ Frequency Data

❏ Yes/No Data

Explanation of Data Collection Procedures:

1: **Maximum Prompting:** Needed physical assistance

2: **Moderate Prompting:** Needed a strategy in Step 5 (a–f)

3: **Minimal Prompting:** Needed teacher proximity

4: **Independent:** No assistance needed

Teaching Procedures:

Use **prompting/fading procedures** and **shaping** to teach Craig to follow directions given by the teacher to the whole class in the following manner:

1. Begin by giving a direction to the whole class while in close proximity to Craig and while making eye contact with him. If he responds, provide **positive reinforcement.**

2. If successful, use **shaping** by giving the next direction in close proximity to Craig but without direct eye contact. If he responds, provide **positive reinforcement.**

3. If successful, the next direction should be given further away from Craig without giving direct eye contact. If he responds, provide **positive reinforcement.**

4. Continue to increase your distance from Craig until he can follow one-step directions given to the whole class from any location in the room.

5. If Craig is not successful after Step 1, attempt any of the following:
   a. Give the direction to Craig one- to- one either before giving the direction to the whole class or after giving the direction to the whole class.
   b. Have Craig restate the direction given to the whole class before having the students comply.
   c. Provide **gestural prompts** such as pointing to indicate what Craig is supposed to do.
   d. Provide a **visual cue** such as a picture showing what he should be doing.
   e. Provide **verbal prompts** such as, "Time to clean up."
   f. Provide **physical prompts** such as holding Craig's hand and walking Craig to the door to line up.

6. If any of the prompts/strategies from Step 5 are used, they should be **faded out** as soon as possible to ensure that Craig does not become dependent on those prompts/strategies in order to follow directions. Use the **shaping** procedure by providing **positive reinforcement** as he gets closer and closer to the ultimate goal of independently following directions.

Figure 7.2. Sample ABA teaching plan: behavior.

delivered. In general, it is best to use natural and social reinforcement as much as possible as opposed to token, activity, and tangible reinforcers.

These sample plans are not the only way to address the objectives indicated. There are many, many ways to teach all skills. Thus there is no right and wrong when it comes to developing teaching procedures. However, the teaching procedures must use behavioral strategies (see Chapter 5). The strategies serve as your toolbox when writing lesson plans. Different individuals will use the strategies in different ways, and that is where the flexibility comes into play. Also, the teaching procedures must be written in an explicit manner so that anyone can implement them in the same way. This is what makes the procedures technological (Chapter 2).

Student	Objective
Ashley	Allow others to join in on what she is playing with or working on in a positive manner (remaining engaged in the activity without running away, yelling, crying, or being aggressive) 80% of the time.

Data Collection Procedures:

☑ Percentage Data

☐ Level of Independence Data

☐ Individualized Rating System

☐ Frequency Data

☐ Yes/No Data

> **Explanation of Data Collection Procedures:**
>
> Each time someone attempts to join Ashley, indicate *correct* if she refrains from displaying negative behaviors and remains engaged in the activity. Indicate *incorrect* if she stops the activity, runs away, yells, cries, or displays aggression. Record the percentage correct by dividing the number of corrects by the total number of opportunities.

Teaching Procedures:

1. If Ashley displays challenging behaviors such as running away, yelling, crying, or aggression when others join her in play or work activities, first set the goal for Ashley to allow the teacher or other adult to join in on the activity.

2. When she is engaged in an activity, approach her by simply sitting with her. If Ashley displays any negative behaviors when you approach her, ignore the negative behaviors until she stops and returns to the activity. During this time do not look at her, talk to her, or indicate any negative emotion. If Ashley does not stop the negative behaviors, **prompt** her to get back on task by using **gestural prompts, verbal prompts,** or **gentle physical guidance** in that order. When she gets back on task, provide **positive reinforcement.** Just be sure that you do not reinforce her escape-motivated behavior by walking away from her if she engages in negative behavior.

3. Once Ashley is able to tolerate you being close by, simply begin to play or work alongside her for the rest of the activity period. Throughout the activity make positive comments and use warm facial expressions to acquire her comfort with your presence.

4. Once Ashley is able to respond positively when the teacher/adult joins in activities with her, begin to implement these same procedures with peers. Be sure to use **peer-mediated intervention** by teaching peers what to do if Ashley displays challenging behaviors and how to work or play alongside her. Be sure to provide **positive reinforcement** to the peers who attempt to join Ashley.

Figure 7.3. Sample ABA teaching plan: social interaction.

Data collection procedures selected for each plan can also be changed. There is never one way to collect data for a specific objective. Choose methods that provide you with the information you want and that you are likely to use effectively and efficiently. Refer to Chapter 6 for a variety of data collection methods that can be used to monitor student progress.

As teachers develop their own ABA teaching plans using this format, they can save them electronically and continually modify and adapt them to meet the needs of specific students. Eventually, a database can be created, with many different teaching plans to choose and alter. If teams of teachers are working together, they can combine their files to create a very large database of ABA teaching plans to draw from when planning ABA interventions in the general education classroom.

Student	Objective
Manuel	Engage in a conversation with the teacher with at least three back-and-forth exchanges during instructional and noninstructional classroom activities.

Data Collection Procedures:

☐ Percentage Data

☐ Level of Independence Data

☐ Individualized Rating System

☑ Frequency Data

☐ Yes/No Data

Explanation of Data Collection Procedures:

0 = no back-and-forth exchanges

1 = usually one back-and-forth exchange

2 = usually two back-and-forth exchanges

3 = always three or more back-and-forth exchanges

Teaching Procedures:

1. Begin by making an open-ended comment to Manuel related to the current activity. For example, if he is unpacking in the morning, you might say, "I like your shirt" when he is removing his coat.

2. Use **time delay** to encourage Manuel to respond to your comment. Accept any response he makes and respond in a positive manner. For example, if you say, "I like your shirt," and he says, "Spider-Man," you can say, "That's a cool picture of Spider-Man on your shirt. What other superheroes do you like?"

3. Use **balanced turn-taking** to gradually increase the length of back-and-forth interactions.

4. If Manuel does not respond to the initial comment, you can repeat the comment or re-phrase the comment to encourage him to respond. If he still does not respond, then ask a more direct question, such as "Who is on your shirt?" as the conversation starter. Just be careful not to only ask questions during this activity. Children need to learn to respond to comments and questions in order to converse.

5. If Manuel doesn't respond after being given a couple of options to respond to a comment and then an option to respond to a question, use additional **prompts** such as fill-ins (e.g., "Your shirt has a picture of _____") or give a choice (e.g., "Do you have Spider-Man or the Hulk on your shirt today?"). Minimize the use of yes/no questions. They can be embedded once Manuel is conversing back and forth, but avoid using them as conversation starters when he is first learning to have a conversation because these are closed-ended responses that often do not lead to more back-and-forth exchanges.

6. Provide **positive reinforcement** when Manuel responds to your comments and questions.

Figure 7.4. Sample ABA teaching plan: communication.

Roles of Professionals, Paraprofessionals, and Parents

When assessing, planning, and implementing ABA interventions in general education classrooms, there need to be collaborative efforts among general education teachers, special education teachers, related services providers, paraprofessionals, and parents. The role that each individual plays will depend on the team as a whole. However, some general guidelines that you can use for aligning roles of team members are suggested in the sections that follow and are summarized in Table 7.1. Of course, you should adjust the roles of your team members based on the experiences they bring to the table and their individual talents.

Student	Objective
Brittany	Follow the morning arrival- to- school routine independently.

Data Collection Procedures:

☑ Percentage Data

☐ Level of Independence Data

☐ Individualized Rating System

☐ Frequency Data

☐ Yes/No Data

> **Explanation of Data Collection Procedures:**
>
> Use the task analysis to document how many steps Brittany completes without assistance. Divide the number of steps performed independently by the total number of steps to get the percentage.

Teaching Procedures:

1. Create a **task analysis** for the arrival routine. Here is an example:
   a. Take off coat.
   b. Hang up coat.
   c. Unpack backpack.
   d. Put homework in bin by the teacher's desk.
   e. Begin morning work.
2. Develop a **self-monitoring** tool for Brittany to use that lists the steps of the arrival routine.
3. Use **forward chaining** (teach the routine in number order starting with step one) to teach Brittany to follow the task analysis.
4. Use **prompting/fading procedures** when Brittany needs help to complete a step on the task analysis. For example, if she gets off task or misses a step of the routine, you can provide a gestural prompt, a visual prompt, a verbal prompt, or provide physical assistance. Just be sure to fade out the prompts you are using as soon as possible.

Figure 7.5. Sample ABA teaching plan: independent functioning.

Table 7.1. Suggested roles

Team member	Role
Special education teacher	Plays the leading role in the assessment, goal setting, development of teaching and data collection procedures, data analysis, training, and support to other members on the team. Provides parents with progress notes about their child's progress related to the ABA interventions.
General education teacher	Works with the special education teacher to gather assessment information, set goals, develop teaching and data collection procedures, and analyze the data. Shares progress and questions with the special education teacher related to the ABA interventions.
Related services providers (speech-language pathologists, occupational therapists, physical therapists)	Work with the special education teacher to gather assessment information, set goals, develop teaching and data collection procedures, and analyze the data for areas related to their expertise. Provide training and support to other members of the team.
Paraprofessionals	Work under the guidance of the special education and general education teachers to assist with implementing the teaching procedures and collecting data.
Parents	Provide information about their child. Communicate priorities. Provide input during the development of teaching procedures based on what they know works best for their child.

Special Education Teacher

In most cases, the special education teacher will serve the leading role when planning ABA interventions for students with ASD in general education classrooms. Of course, there may be cases in which another professional serves that role, depending on the training and experiences of the team members. As the lead person, the special education teacher (or other professional) will facilitate the team's activities throughout the assessment, goal-setting, teaching procedures development, implementation, and progress-monitoring phases. This does not mean that the special education teacher does all of the actual work. During the assessment and goal-setting phases, the special education teacher should facilitate team discussions to determine what assessments will be done, how they will be done, and who will do them and then reconvene with the team to analyze the results of the assessments to select appropriate goals for the student. When developing teaching procedures, the special education teacher should work collaboratively with the general education teacher to design teaching procedures that are appropriate for the student within the context of the general education classroom. This is a perfect opportunity to provide training to the general education teacher on specific strategies that are used within the teaching plans. When it is time to implement the plans, the special education teacher should provide ongoing support to the general education teacher, and possibly paraprofessionals, to ensure the strategies are being implemented as suggested. Although the general education teacher will be the primary person responsible for data collection, the special education teacher should regularly meet with the general education teacher to monitor progress and make data-based instructional decisions (see Chapter 6). The special education teacher should communicate regularly with parents to inform them of their child's progress and to address questions and/or concerns. In some situations, the general education teacher may take on more of the responsibility for communicating with parents, but the team members should determine whether that will be the case.

General Education Teacher

The general education teacher must be actively involved in the assessment, goal-setting, and teaching procedures development phases to be able to implement the ABA interventions within the classroom. Very few teachers would have "buy-in" if someone just tells them what they should work on and how they should teach. The teaching style of the general education teacher and the context of the classroom should be considered when developing ABA intervention plans. This cannot be done adequately without the general education teacher being actively engaged during all assessment and planning phases. Once the interventions are being implemented, the general education teacher should seek support from the special education teacher as needed. Most general education teachers do not have much training in understanding ASD or ABA. Therefore, it is not expected that implementation will come easily without the need for ongoing support. If a paraprofessional will be assisting with the implementation of the ABA interventions, the general education teacher should provide ongoing training and support to that individual to ensure that the teaching and data collection procedures are being implemented accurately. The special education teacher can also assist with training paraprofessionals; however, it is the general education teacher who will be able to provide the most support to paraprofessionals because they will work alongside one another much more often. The general education teacher will be responsible for the bulk of the data collection. This is why data collection procedures should be selected that are easy to gather (see Chapter 6). Data should be reviewed regularly in collaboration with the special education teacher to monitor progress and make instructional decisions. Depending on whether or not the special education teacher is responsible for communicating with families, the general education teacher may be the key person who will communicate with families. It is important for families to be informed about the progress their child is making, but they do not need two different people delivering the same information.

In classrooms that have a general education teacher and special education teacher working together for all or part of the day, the role of the special education teacher will also include implementing the ABA interventions, collecting data, and training and supporting any paraprofessionals who may also be working in the classroom. This does not mean that the general education teacher will not implement the interventions, collect data, and support paraprofessionals, but the responsibility will be shared between the two teachers. Although this is the ideal situation, budgeting issues often do not allow co-teaching to occur.

Related Services Professionals

Speech-language pathologists, occupational therapists, physical therapists, and guidance counselors may be involved in planning and implementing ABA interventions. These professionals should have opportunities to be a part of the assessment, goal-setting, and teaching procedures development phases. The best-case scenario is one in which these related services providers give support to the general education teacher and the students with ASD within the general education classroom as opposed to pulling the students out of the classroom. This will allow them to model strategies for the general education teacher and to assist with implementing interventions within the natural context of the general education classroom.

Paraprofessionals

The misuse of paraprofessionals in general education classrooms is well-documented (Downing, Ryndak, & Clark, 2000; Giangreco & Broer, 2007). Paraprofessionals frequently are relied on too much for the instruction of students with ASD in general education classrooms. This leads to many negative impacts, as was discussed in Chapter 1. Thus it is important to utilize paraprofessionals in an appropriate manner when they are involved in implementing ABA interventions. First, paraprofessionals should not be the ones solely responsible for implementing the ABA interventions. That responsibility falls on the general education teacher. However, with support from the general education teacher, there are some objectives for which paraprofessionals can provide instruction to supplement what is being provided by the general education teacher and to increase the learning opportunities for the students. Paraprofessionals must work under the guidance of the general education teacher, implement teaching and data collection procedures as instructed, and be sure to ask for assistance and support when needed.

Parents

Parents should be involved through all phases of planning and implementing ABA interventions in general education classrooms as well. They have valuable information to provide during the assessment process, their priorities should be addressed when selecting goals, and they may have suggestions to offer for teaching strategies that have worked well or have not worked well with their child in the past. They should have opportunities to ask questions, review data, and learn how to implement interventions at home as appropriate. If permission for videotaping is granted, the general education teacher can take short video clips of the ABA interventions being implemented to share with parents at meetings and for training purposes.

Chapter Summary

Before beginning any assessment, goal setting, or development of ABA teaching plans, plan a team meeting to align the roles each team member will play throughout the process. The suggestions presented in this chapter can be used as a guide, but each team will individualize the roles of their members as they see fit. Similarly, the format for developing ABA teaching plans presented in this chapter can and should be adjusted to meet your students' needs and the preferences of your team members. However, whatever format you choose to use, it is important to include the following:

- Objectives that are observable, measurable, functional, and developmentally appropriate
- Data collection procedures
- Technological and conceptual teaching procedures

Including each of these components allows teams to address the dimensions of ABA (Baer, Wolf, & Risley, 1968) when planning interventions for the general education classroom.

Now, your team is ready to put all of this together to plan ABA interventions to address the needs of your students with ASD in general education classrooms. Does this mean extra work for everyone? Sure it does, but the benefits you will see as your students reach mastery of their objectives and learn how to fully participate in their classrooms will certainly be worth your efforts. ABA teaching in general education classrooms provides the explicit instruction students with ASD often need to reach their full potential and to take advantage of all of the wonderful, natural learning opportunities that these classrooms provide. Students with ASD can be successfully included in general education classrooms with collaborative efforts among general education teachers, special education teachers, related services providers, paraprofessionals, and parents to plan and implement ABA interventions to address their individual learning needs.

References

American Psychiatric Association. (2000). *Diagnostic and statistical manual of mental disorders* (4th ed., text rev.). Washington, DC: Author.

Baer, D.M., Wolf, M.M., & Risley, T.F. (1968). Some current dimensions of applied behavior analysis. *Journal of Applied Behavior Analysis, 1,* 91–97.

Baer, D.M., Wolf, M.M., & Risley, T.F. (1987). Some still-current dimensions of applied behavior analysis. *Journal of Applied Behavior Analysis, 20,* 313–327.

Bailey, J.S., & Burch, M.R. (2002). *Research methods in applied behavior analysis.* Thousand Oaks, CA: Sage Publications.

Baldwin, D.A. (1995). Understanding the link between joint attention and language. In C. Moore & P.J. Dunham (Eds.), *Joint attention: Its origins and role in development* (pp. 131–158). Hillsdale, NJ: Erlbaum.

Bellini, S. (2006). *Building social relationships: A systematic approach to teaching social interaction skills to children and adolescents with autism spectrum disorders and other social difficulties.* Shawnee Mission, KS: Autism Asperger Publishing.

Bellini, S., Akullian, J., & Hopf, A. (2007). Increasing social engagement in young children with autism spectrum disorders using video self-modeling. *School Psychology Review, 36*(1), 80–90.

Bianco, M., Carothers, D.E., & Smiley, L.R. (2009). Gifted students with Asperger syndrome: Strategies for strengths-based programming. *Intervention in School and Clinic, 44*(4), 206–215.

Bradshaw, C.P., Reinke, W.M., Brown, L.D., Bevans, K.B., & Leaf, P.J. (2008). Implementation of school-wide Positive Behavioral Interventions and Supports (PBIS) in elementary schools: Observations from a randomized trial [Report]. *Education & Treatment of Children, 31*(1), 1–26.

Breen, C., Haring, T.G., Pitts-Conway, V., & Gaylord-Ross, R. (1985). The training and generalization of social interaction during break time at two job sites in the natural environment. *Journal of The Association for Persons with Severe Handicaps, 10,* 41–50.

Broer, S.M., Doyle, M.B., & Giangreco, M.F. (2005). Perspectives of students with intellectual disabilities about their experiences with paraprofessional support. *Exceptional Children, 71*(4), 415–430.

Buffington, D.M., Krantz, P.J., McClannahan, L.E., & Poulson, C.L. (1998). Procedures for teaching appropriate gestural communication skills to children with autism. *Journal of Autism and Developmental Disorders, 28*(6), 535–545.

Buron, K.D., & Curtis, M. (2003). *The incredible 5-point scale: Assisting students with autism spectrum disorders in understanding social interactions and controlling their emotional responses.* Shawnee Mission, KS: Autism Asperger Publishing.

Cautilli, J., & Dziewolska, H. (2005). Brief report: Can contingent imitation reinforce truck lifting in a three-month-old infant? *The Behavior Analyst Today, 6*(4), 229–230.

Chan, J.M., & O'Reilly, M.F. (2008). A Social Stories intervention package for students with autism in inclusive classroom settings. *Journal of Applied Behavior Analysis, 41*(3), 405–409.

Chandler-Olcott, K., & Kluth, P. (2009). Why everyone benefits from including students with autism in literacy classrooms. *The Reading Teacher, 62*(7), 548–557.

Constantino, J.N., Davis, S.A., Todd, R.D., Schindler, M.K., Gross, M.M., Brophy, S.L., et al. (2003). Validation of a brief quantitative measure of autistic traits: Comparison of the Social Responsiveness Scale with the Autism Diagnostic Interview–Revised. *Journal of Autism and Developmental Disorders, 33*(4), 427–433.

Cooper, J.O., Heron, T.E., & Heward, W.L. (1987). *Applied behavior analysis.* Englewood Cliffs, NJ: Prentice Hall.

Coyle, C., & Cole, P. (2004). A videotaped self-modeling and self-monitoring treatment program to treat off-task behavior in children with autism. *Journal of Intellectual and Developmental Disability, 29*(1), 3–15.

Daniels, V.I. (1999). The assessment maze: Making instructional decisions about alternative assessments for students with disabilities. *Preventing School Failure, 43*(4), 171–178.

Davis, C.A., Brady, M.P., Hamilton, R., McEvoy, M.A., & Williams, R.E. (1994). Effects of high-probability requests on the social interactions of young children with severe disabilities. *Journal of Applied Behavior Analysis, 27,* 619–637.

Diehl, S.F., Ford, C.S., & Federico, J. (2005). The communication journey of a fully included child with an autism spectrum disorder. *Topics in Language Disorders, 25*(4), 375–387.

Dipipi, C.M., Jitendra, A.K., & Miller, J.A. (2001). Reducing repetitive speech: Effects of strategy instruction. *Preventing School Failure, 45*(4), 177–181.

DiSalvo, C.A., & Oswald, D.P. (2002). Peer-mediated interventions to increase the social interaction of children with autism: Consideration of peer expectancies. *Focus on Autism and Other Developmental Disabilities, 17*(4), 198–207.

Downing, J.E., Ryndak, D.L., & Clark, D. (2000). Paraeducators in inclusive classrooms. *Remedial and Special Education, 21,* 171–181.

Dowrick, P. (1999). A review of self-modeling and related interventions. *Applied and Preventive Psychology, 8,* 23–39.

Ganz, J. (2008). Self-monitoring across age and ability levels: Teaching students to implement their own positive behavioral interventions. *Preventing School Failure, 53*(1), 39–48.

Gazdag, G., & Warren, S.F. (2000). Effects of adult contingent imitation on development of young children's vocal imitation. *Journal of Early Intervention, 23,* 24–35.

Giangreco, M.F., & Broer, S.M. (2007). School-based screening to determine overreliance on paraprofessionals. *Focus on Autism and Other Developmental Disabilities, 22*(3), 149–158.

Gray, C.A., & Garand, J.D. (1993). Social Stories: Improving responses of students with autism with accurate social information. *Focus on Autistic Behavior, 8,* 1–10.

Gresham, F.M., & MacMillan, D.L. (1998). Early intervention projects: Can its claims be substantiated and its effects replicated? *Journal of Autism and Developmental Disorders, 28,* 5–13.

Halle, J.W., Marshall, A.M., & Spradlin, J.E. (1979). Time delay: A technique to increase language use and facilitate generalization in retarded children. *Journal of Applied Behavior Analysis, 14,* 389–409.

Hanley, G., Piazza, C.C., Fisher, W.W., & Maglieri, K.A. (2005). On the effectiveness of and preference for punishment and extinction components of function-based interventions. *Journal of Applied Behavior Analysis, 38,* 51–65.

Hargrove, L.J., Church, K.L., Yssel, N., & Koch, K. (2002). Curriculum-based assessment: Reading and state academic standards. *Preventing School Failure, 46*(4), 148–151.

Haring, T.G., & Ryndak, D. (1994). Strategies and instructional procedures to promote social interactions and relationships. In E.C. Cipani & F. Spooner (Eds.), *Curricular and instructional approaches for persons with severe disabilities* (pp. 289–321). Boston: Allyn & Bacon.

Hart, B.M., & Risley, T.R. (1975). Incidental teaching of language in preschool. *Journal of Applied Behavior Analysis, 8,* 411–420.

Hemmings, A. (2000). The hidden curriculum corridor. *High School Journal, 83*(2), 1–10.

Horner, R.H. (1994). Functional assessment: Contributions and future directions. *Journal of Applied Behavior Analysis, 27,* 401–404.

Individuals with Disabilities Education Improvement Act (IDEA) of 2004, PL 108-446, 20 U.S.C. §§ 1400 *et seq.*

Jones, E.A., & Carr, E.G. (2004). Joint attention in children with autism: Theory and intervention. *Focus on Autism & Other Developmental Disabilities, 19,* 13–26.

Jung, S., Sainato, D.M., & Davis, C.A. (2008). Using high-probability request sequences to increase social interactions in young children with autism. *Journal of Early Intervention, 30*(3), 163–187.

Kates-McElrath, K., & Axelrod, S. (2006). Behavioral intervention for autism: A distinction between two behavior analytic approaches. *The Behavior Analyst Today, 7*(2), 242–252.

King-Sears, M.E. (2008). Facts and fallacies: Differentiation and the general education curriculum for students with special educational needs. *Support for Learning, 23*(2), 55–62.

Kluth, P., & Schwarz, P. (2008). *"Just give him the whale!" 20 ways to use fascinations, areas of expertise, and strengths to support students with autism.* Baltimore: Paul H. Brookes Publishing Co.

Koegel, L.K., & Koegel, R.L. (1995). Motivating communication in children with autism. In E. Schopler & G.B. Mesibov (Eds.), *Learning and cognition in autism* (pp. 73–87). New York: Kluwer Academic/Plenum.

Koegel, L.K., Koegel, R.L., Harrower, J.K., & Carter, C.M. (1999). Pivotal Response Intervention, I: Overview of approach. *Journal of Applied Behavior Analysis, 25,* 341–354.

Koegel, L.K., Koegel, R.L., Hurley, C., & Frea, W.D. (1992). Improving social skills and disruptive behavior in children with autism through self-management. *Journal of Applied Behavior Analysis, 25,* 341–353.

Koegel, R.L., & Koegel, L.K. (2006). *Pivotal Response Treatments for autism: Communication, social & academic achievement.* Baltimore: Paul H. Brookes Publishing Co.

Landa, R. (2007). Early communication development and intervention for children with autism. *Mental Retardation and Developmental Disabilities Research Reviews, 13,* 16–25.

Lawrence-Brown, D. (2004). Differentiated instruction: Inclusive strategies for standards-based learning that benefit the whole class. *American Secondary Education, 32,* 34–62.

Layer, S.A., Hanley, G.P., Heal, N.A., & Tiger, J.H. (2008). Determining individual preschoolers' preferences in a group arrangement. *Journal of Applied Behavior Analysis, 41,* 25–37.

Lovaas, O.I. (1977). *The autistic child: Language development through behavior modification.* New York: Irvington Press.

Lovaas, O.I. (1987). Behavioral treatment and normal educational and intellectual functioning in young autistic children. *Journal of Counseling and Clinical Psychology, 55,* 3–9.

Lovaas, O.I. (2003). *Teaching individuals with developmental delays: Basic intervention techniques.* Austin, TX: PRO-ED.

Lovaas, O.I., Ackerman, A., Alexander, D., Firestone, P., Perkins, J., & Young, D. (1981). *Teaching developmentally disabled children: The ME book.* Austin, TX: PRO-ED.

MacDonald, J.D., & Carroll, J.Y. (1992). A social partnership model for assessing early communication development: An intervention model for preconversational children. *Language, Speech, and Hearing Services in Schools, 23,* 113–124.

MacDonald, R., Anderson, J., Dube, W.V., Geckeler, A., Green, G., Holcomb, W., et al. (2006). Behavioral assessment of joint attention: A methodological report. *Research in Developmental Disabilities, 27,* 138–150.

Maurice, C., Green, G., & Luce, S. (Eds.). (1996). *Behavioral intervention for young children with autism: A manual for parents and professionals.* Austin, TX: PRO-ED.

McGee, G.G., Almeida, M.C., Sulzer-Azaroff, B., & Feldman, R.S., (1992). Promoting reciprocal interactions via peer incidental teaching. *Journal of Applied Behavior Analysis, 25*(1), 117–126.

McGee, G.G., Krantz, P.J., & McClannahan, L.E. (1985). The facilitative effects of incidental teaching on preposition use by autistic children. *Journal of Applied Behavior Analysis, 18,* 17–31.

McGee, G.G., Morrier, J.J., & Daly, T. (1999). An incidental teaching approach to early intervention for toddlers with autism. *Journal of The Association for Persons with Severe Handicaps, 24,* 133–146.

McGraw-Hill. (1992). *Distar arithmetic 1992.* New York: Author.

McGraw-Hill. (1999). *Language for learning 1999.* New York: Author.

McGraw-Hill. (2008). *Reading mastery signature edition 2008.* New York: Author.

Morrison, L., Kamps, D., Garcia, J., & Parker, D. (2001). Peer mediation and monitoring strategies to improve initiations and social skills for students with autism. *Journal of Positive Behavior Interventions, 3*(4), 237–250.

Mundy, P. (1995). Joint attention and social-emotional approach behavior in children with autism. *Development and Psychopathology, 7,* 63–82.

Mundy, P., Sigman, M., & Kasari, C. (1990). A longitudinal study of joint attention and language development in autistic children. *Journal of Autism and Developmental Disorders, 20,* 115–128.

Murawski, W.W., & Hughes, C.E. (2009). Response to intervention, collaboration, and co-teaching: A logical combination for successful systemic change. *Preventing School Failure, 53*(4), 267–277.

Myles, B.S., Simpson, R.L. (2001). Understanding the hidden curriculum: An essential social skill for children and youth with Asperger syndrome. *Intervention in School and Clinic, 36*(5), 279–286.

Myles, B.S., Trautman, M.L., & Schelvan, R.L. (2004). *The hidden curriculum: Practical solutions for understanding unstated rules in social situations.* Shawnee Mission, KS: Autism Asperger Publishing.

National Research Council. (2001). *Educating children with autism.* Washington, DC: National Academies Press.

No Child Left Behind Act of 2001, PL 107-110, 115 Stat. 1425, 20 U.S.C. §§ 6301 *et seq.*

Noonan, M.J., & McCormick, L. (2006). *Young children with disabilities in natural environments.* Baltimore: Paul H. Brookes Publishing Co.

Odom, S.L., Deklyen, M., & Jenkins, J.R. (1984). Integrating handicapped and non-handicapped preschoolers: Developmental impact on non-handicapped children. *Exceptional Children, 51*(1), 41–48.

O'Neill, R.E., Horner, R.H., Albin, R.W., Sprague, J.R., Storey, D., & Newton, J.S. (1997). *Functional assessment and program development for problem behavior: A practical handbook* (2nd ed.). Pacific Grove, CA: Brooks/Cole.

Partington, J.W., & Sundberg, M.L. (1998). *The assessment of basic language and learning skills: An assessment, curriculum guide, and skills tracking system for children with autism and other developmental disabilities.* Pleasant Hill, CA: Behavior Analysts.

Pierce, K.L., & Schreibman, L. (1994). Teaching daily living skills to children with autism in unsupervised settings through pictorial self-management. *Journal of Applied Behavior Analysis, 27*(3), 471–481.

Pierce, K.L., & Schreibman, L. (1995). Increasing complex social behaviors in children with autism: Effects of peer-implemented pivotal response training. *Journal of Applied Behavior Analysis, 28*(3), 285–295.

Pierce, K.L., & Schreibman, L. (1997). Multiple peer use of pivotal response training to increase social behaviors of classmates with autism: Results from trained and untrained peers. *Journal of Applied Behavior Analysis, 30*(1), 157–160.

Quill, K.A. (2000). *Do-watch-listen-say: Social and communication intervention for children with autism.* Baltimore: Paul H. Brookes Publishing Co.

Robertson, J., Green, K., Alper, S., Schloss, P.J., & Kohler, F. (2003). Using a peer-mediated intervention to facilitate children's participation in inclusive childcare activities. *Education & Treatment of Children, 26*(2), 182–197.

Sansosti, F.J., & Powell-Smith, K.A. (2008). Using computer-presented social stories and video models to increase the social communication skills of children with high-functioning autism spectrum disorders. *Journal of Positive Behavior Interventions, 10*(3), 162–178.

Scott, T.M., & Caron, D.B. (2005). Conceptualizing functional behavior assessment as prevention practice within positive behavior support systems. *Preventing School Failure, 50*(1), 13–21.

Skinner, B.F. (1957). *Verbal behavior.* Engelwood Cliffs, NJ: Prentice Hall.

Skokut, M., Robinson, S., Openden, D., & Jimerson, S.R. (2008). Promoting the social and cognitive competence of children with autism: Interventions at school. *The California School Psychologist, 13,* 93–108.

Spradlin, J.E., & Seigel, G.M. (1982). Language training in natural and clinical environments. *Journal of Speech and Hearing Disorders, 47,* 2–6.

Staub, D., & Peck, C. (1994). What are the outcomes for nondisabled students? *Educational Leadership, 52*(4), 36–40.

Stokes, T.F., & Baer, D.M. (1977). An implicit technology of generalization. *Journal of Applied Behavior Analysis, 10,* 349–367.

Stribling, P., Rae, J., & Dickerson, P. (2007). Two forms of spoken repetition in a girl with autism. *International Journal of Language and Communication Disorders, 42*(4), 427–444.

Sugai, G., Horner, R., Dunlap, G., Hieneman, M., Lewis, T., Nelson, M., Scott, T., et al. (1999). Applying positive behavioral support and functional behavior assessment in schools. Technical Assistance Guide 1, Version 1.4.3. Washington, DC: Center on Positive Behavioral Interventions and Support.

Sundberg, M.L., & Michael, J. (2001). The benefits of Skinner's analysis of verbal behavior on children with autism. *Behavior Modification, 25,* 698–724.

Swaggart, B., Gangon, E., Bock, S.J., Earles, T.L., Quinn, C., Myles, B.S., et al. (1995). Using social stories to teach social and behavioral skills to children with autism. *Focus on Autistic Behavior, 10,* 1–16.

Thiemann, K.S., Goldstein, H. (2001). Social stories, written text cues, and video feedback: Effects on social communication of children with autism. *Journal of Applied Behavior Analysis, 34,* 425–446.

Tomlinson, C. (1999). *The differentiated classroom: Responding to the needs of all learners.* Alexandria, VA: Association for Supervision and Curriculum Development.

Weiss, M.J. (2005). Comprehensive ABA programs: Integrating and evaluating the implementation of varied instructional approaches. *The Behavior Analyst Today, 6*(4), 249–256.

Wolery, M., Ault, M.J., & Doyle, P.M. (1992). *Teaching students with moderate to severe disabilities.* White Plains, NY: Longman.

Zanolli, K.M., Paden, P., & Cox, K. (1997). Teaching prosocial behavior to typically developing toddlers. *Journal of Behavioral Education, 7*(3), 373–391.

Resources

· ·

Applied Behavior Analysis

Alberto, P.A., & Troutman, A.C. (2008). *Applied behavior analysis for teachers* (8th ed.). Upper Saddle River, NJ: Pearson/Merrill Prentice Hall.

Barbera, M.L. (2007). *The Verbal Behavior approach: How to teach children with autism and related disorders.* Philadelphia: Jessica Kingsley.

Cooper, J.O., Heron, T.E., & Heward, W.L. (2007). *Applied behavior analysis* (2nd ed.). Upper Saddle River, NJ: Pearson/Merrill Prentice Hall.

Duker, P., Didden, R., & Sigafoos, J. (2004). *One-to-one training: Instructional procedures for learners with developmental disabilities.* Austin, TX: PRO-ED.

Harris, S.L., & Weiss, M.J. (2007). *Right from the start: Behavioral intervention for young children with autism.* Bethesda, MD: Woodbine House.

Kearney, A.J. (2007). *Understanding applied behavior analysis: An introduction to ABA for parents, teachers, and other professionals.* Philadelphia: Jessica Kingsley.

Koegel, R.L., & Koegel, L.K. (2006). *Pivotal Response Treatments for autism: Communication, social & academic achievement.* Baltimore: Paul H. Brookes Publishing Co.

Lovaas, O.I. (2002). *Teaching individuals with developmental delays: Basic intervention techniques.* Austin, TX: PRO-ED.

Maurice, K. (1996). *Behavioral intervention for young children with autism: A manual for parents and professionals.* Austin, TX: PRO-ED.

Including Students with ASD

Fein, D., & Dunn, M.A. (2007). *Autism in your classroom: A general educator's guide to students with autism spectrum disorders.* Bethesda, MD: Woodbine House.

Kluth, P. (2003). *You're going to love this kid! Teaching students with autism in the inclusive classroom.* Baltimore: Paul H. Brookes Publishing Co.

Wagner, S. (1998). *Inclusive programming for elementary students with autism.* Arlington, TX: Future Horizons.

Wagner, S. (2002). *Inclusive programming for middle school students with autism/Asperger's syndrome.* Arlington, TX: Future Horizons.

Websites

Autism Internet Modules: http://www.autisminternetmodules.org/—Provides free training modules to promote a greater understanding of ASD and to promote achievement, full participation, respect, and equality of individuals with ASD

Autism Pro: http://www.autismpro.com—Works with school districts, early intervention providers, and governments to supplement quality programs

Autism Society: http://www.autism-society.org—Autism information and resources for parents and professionals

Autism Speaks: http://www.autismspeaks.org—Autism information and resources for parents and professionals

Autism Teaching Tools: http://www.autismteachingtools.com/—Provides ways to help learners with ASD

Cambridge Center for Behavioral Studies: Autism and ABA: http://www.behavior.org/autism/—Provides scientifically validated information about the causes of autism and explanation of ABA approaches

Paula Kluth: http://www.paulakluth.com—Promotes inclusive schooling and exploring positive ways of supporting students with autism and other disabilities

Polyxo.com: http://www.polyxo.com/—Provides a variety of instructional techniques and philosophies for teaching students with autism and other related developmental disorders

Study Guide

· ·

Chapter 1
Students with Autism in General Education Classrooms

1. Think about at least three different students with ASD. Discuss the characteristics of each student, including the student's strengths as well as social impairments, communication impairments, and restricted interests and repetitive behaviors. How are these three students similar? How are they different?

2. Discuss the benefits for students with ASD when they are included in general education classrooms. How do you think their typically developing peers benefit when they are included? What are the benefits for general education teachers, special education teachers, and families of children with ASD?

3. Consider all of the barriers to including students with ASD in general education classrooms in your school. Discuss how each barrier can be overcome.

4. For students with ASD to be successfully included in general education classrooms, teachers need to utilize positive behavioral supports and differentiated instruction and provide opportunities for active engagement throughout the school day. Consider the classrooms in your school. Are there classrooms that already have these things in place? How much support would the teachers in your school need to have these things in place? Devise a plan for working toward all classrooms having these things in place.

5. Consider how paraprofessionals working with students with ASD in general education classrooms in your schools are currently being utilized. Would you consider their current responsibilities and duties appropriate? What do you think needs to change about the supports they provide and receive?

6. Discuss the rationale for using ABA teaching procedures in general education classrooms to meet the needs of students with ASD. Do you think students with ASD are the only students who would benefit from some explicit instruction within the school day?

Chapter 2
Understanding ABA

1. Discuss how ABA came into existence. What are the historical roots?

2. In your own words, discuss the meaning of ABA. Considering the meaning of ABA, how can it be useful for students with ASD in general education classrooms?

3. Consider an intervention you are currently implementing with a student in a general education classroom. Which of the seven dimensions of ABA are you already addressing? What changes or additions would you need to make for the intervention to be considered an ABA intervention?

4. If you are going to implement interventions to teach a student with ASD how to request help during independent work activities, how can you address all of the dimensions of ABA?

5. Provide an example for how you can use DTT in the general education classroom to teach a student how to respond when greeted by a peer.

6. How do PRT and IT differ from DTT? How do you think you might use PRT or IT to teach a child to request desired items in the general education classroom?

7. The author does not recommend that teachers select a specific application of ABA such as DTT, PRT, IT, or AVB as the sole intervention for students with ASD in the general education classroom. Instead, the strategies utilized within these approaches can be used in a variety of ways, along with other behavioral strategies, to develop quality ABA interventions. Why do you think the author suggests this for ABA in inclusive classrooms?

Chapter 3
Assessment for Planning ABA Interventions

1. Why is it important to conduct assessments before writing goals for ABA interventions?

2. How can ABA interventions be aligned with a student's IEP goals?

3. Think about a student with ASD with whom you are currently working. Are there goals on this student's IEP that the student is not achieving? If so, which of these goals do you think would be best met through ABA interventions?

4. Discuss the importance for conducting assessments of the strengths and interests of students with ASD. How much of this is currently done as part of your assessments and instructional planning activities?

5. Plan a strengths and interest assessment for a student who is nonverbal. Consider multiple ways to obtain this information from the actual student as opposed to just relying on interviews with adults.

6. Many teachers (and parents) have difficulty remaining positive when developing a present level of performance. Consider a student with ASD whom you are currently teaching. Informally discuss all of the things the child *can do* related to communication, social interaction, behavior, academics, and independent functioning.

7. What are some special considerations that should be made when conducting functional behavior assessments with students with ASD?

8. Why is it important to assess the priorities of parents? Why is it important to assess the priorities of general education teachers?

Time to Practice: Select a student with ASD who you feel would benefit from the use of ABA interventions in the general education classroom. Decide which domains the interventions should address (academics, behavior, social, communication, and/or independent functioning). Conduct and interpret assessments to determine the student's present level of performance for each domain you would like to address. Determine parent and general education teacher priorities for each of these areas as well.

Chapter 4
Goal Setting

1. How can you work collaboratively with your team members to set goals for ABA interventions for students with ASD in general education classrooms? How can you ensure all parties are involved (parents, general education teachers, special education teachers, and related services providers)?

2. Goals for IEPs and goals for ABA interventions must meet the same criteria (functional, developmentally appropriate, observable, measurable, and positively stated). Examine some current IEP goals for your students with ASD to determine which ones do and do not meet these criteria.

3. Select an annual goal from one of your student's IEPs for which you would like to develop ABA interventions because the student is not making adequate progress. Does the goal need to be broken down into a set of subskills or short-term objectives to address the student's current skill level? If so, create a list of skills required to meet the annual goal that can be addressed one by one with ABA interventions.

4. What are some skills that would be appropriate to teach one of your students with ASD using ABA interventions in the general education classroom that are not currently on the student's IEP?

5. There are many "hidden curriculum" skills for which students with ASD require explicit instruction to learn. Think about three different students with ASD. Come up with a list of hidden curriculum skills that may require ABA interventions for each student.

Time to Practice: Now that you have conducted the assessments for one of your students to determine present levels of performance and parent and general education teacher priorities, work collaboratively to select goals for ABA interventions. Make sure the goals are written in a manner that they meet the criteria discussed in Chapter 4.

Chapter 5
Developing ABA Teaching Procedures

1. Consider a student with ASD in your classroom. What are some skills that the student has but is not performing fluently, consistently, or in a generalized manner? How would the student benefit from ABA teaching procedures that focus on skill performance? What are some skills the student does not have and would require explicit teaching procedures for skill acquisition?

2. What types of positive reinforcement are commonly used in your classroom? Think of some examples of how you have used tangible reinforcement, activity reinforcement, token reinforcement, social reinforcement, and natural reinforcement.

3. Most teachers need to work on increasing their use of time delay with students with ASD to prevent them from becoming prompt-dependent. Are there times you can think of when, if you provided the wait time necessary, the student may have responded without the need for further assistance?

4. In schools, teachers do need to be quite directive some of the time. However, there are times when they can follow the lead of their students with ASD to provide explicit instruction during an activity in which the student is currently engaged. Think of some examples when you can follow the lead of a student with ASD within the general education classroom to enhance teaching and learning.

5. How can you use behavioral momentum to improve the conversational skills of a student with ASD during ongoing classroom activities?

6. How can you use embedded discrete trials to teach a student how to ask for help?

7. How would you go about using peer-mediated interventions to teach a student to engage in joint play during recess?

Time to Practice: Now that you have set goals for the student you selected, it is time to develop ABA teaching procedures for each goal. Make sure the procedures are technological (written in a manner so that the intervention can be replicated in the same manner by many) and conceptual (use behavioral strategies such as the ones explained in Chapter 5).

Chapter 6
Data Collection and Analysis

1. Discuss why it is important to collect data when implementing ABA interventions in general education classrooms.

2. Review a student's IEP. What are the current data collection procedures being used to monitor the student's progress? How can the data collection happen more often or in an easier fashion using one or more of the procedures explained in Chapter 6?

3.   Think about some possible goals that you would use percentage data for progress monitoring. What about level of independence data, individualized rating systems, frequency data, and yes/no data?

4.   How often should data be collected when implementing ABA interventions in general education classrooms?

5.   Discuss what should be done if the data indicate that a student is not making adequate progress on a specific objective.

Time to Practice: You have goals selected and teaching procedures developed. It is now time to determine how data will be collected for each objective. Try to use several different data collection procedures so that you get some practice with each of them. You can use the sample data collection sheets provided in Chapter 6, or you may need to modify them to fit your specific needs.

Chapter 7
Putting It All Together

1.   Discuss whether there is anything you would change or add to the ABA teaching plan template provided to best meet your needs.

2.   Review the sample lesson plans provided in Chapter 7 and Appendixes A–E. Choose one that would be appropriate for one of your students. What would you change about the teaching procedures or data collection procedures?

3.   Discuss some ideas you have about roles various individuals should play when assessing, planning, and implementing ABA interventions in general education classrooms for students with ASD that may differ from the suggestions made in Chapter 7.

Time to Practice: Hold a meeting with your team to determine the roles that each of you will play when planning ABA interventions for students with ASD. Also, you now have a complete ABA intervention plan for one student with ASD. It's time to begin implementing the interventions, collecting data, and monitoring progress. Ready, set, go!

Academic Teaching Plans

OBJECTIVE: Participate in cooperative learning activities with peers independently

DATA COLLECTION PROCEDURES:

- ☐ Percentage Data
- ☑ Level of Independence Data
- ☐ Individualized Rating System
- ☐ Frequency Data
- ☐ Yes/No Data

> EXPLANATION OF
> DATA COLLECTION PROCEDURES:
>
> **1. Maximum Prompting:**
> Needed continuous teacher support
>
> **2. Moderate Prompting:**
> Needed some teacher support
>
> **3. Minimal Prompting:**
> Needed very little teacher support
>
> **4. Independent:**
> No teacher support needed

TEACHING PROCEDURES:

1. Provide **explicit instructions** to the class regarding the expectations for the cooperative learning activity.

2. Include in the instructions that one of the goals for the group is to ensure that all students participate throughout the activity. Involve the students in a discussion to think about ways to encourage a peer to participate if that individual gets off task. Write the ideas on the board, number them, and leave them up during the cooperative learning activity as a **visual support.**

3. If the student is expected to have great difficulty remaining engaged with the group, an adult should facilitate the group activity. The adult facilitating the group activity should focus on providing support to the peers so they learn how to engage the student in the task.

4. The adult can **prompt** the peers by holding up the number of fingers that correlates to the idea on the board. For example, if the

Number 3 idea says to ask the student a question, the adult can look at the peer and hold up three fingers to encourage the peer to ask the student a question to increase involvement.

5. Although the adult facilitating the group may need to provide some direct **prompting/fading** procedures to the student during the activity, it is important to transfer that type of redirection to the peers as quickly as possible through **peer-mediated interventions.**

6. Provide **positive reinforcement** during the cooperative learning activity to the student when the student is participating appropriately in the activity. This can be done through **specific praise, token reinforcement,** or **natural reinforcement** (the student receives positive social interactions from the peers in the group). Also be sure to provide positive reinforcement to the peers using peer-mediated intervention strategies to involve the student in the activity.

Note: Be sure to have developmentally appropriate expectations for the student throughout the group activity. Ensure that the student has the skills needed to fulfill the expectations. This means you may need to adjust the expectations for the student to increase participation opportunities.

STUDENT: Olivia

OBJECTIVE: Define five content area vocabulary words each week with 80% accuracy

DATA COLLECTION PROCEDURES:

☑ Percentage Data
☐ Level of Independence Data
☐ Individualized Rating System
☐ Frequency Data
☐ Yes/No Data

> EXPLANATION OF
> DATA COLLECTION PROCEDURES:
> At the end of the week, provide Olivia with the five vocabulary words on a piece of paper. Olivia must write a definition for each vocabulary word in her own words. Record and graph the percentage correct.

TEACHING PROCEDURES:

1. Introduce a new vocabulary word within the context of an instructional lesson. For example, if the word is *evaporate,* introduce the word during a hands-on science lesson that teaches the concept of evaporation.

2. When you introduce the word, ask the class if anyone can tell you what evaporate means. If you get a correct answer, repeat the correct answer to the class and say, "Now who can tell me what evaporate means?"

3. If Olivia's hand goes up, call on her. Provide **specific academic and/or social praise** if the response is correct by saying something such as, "That's exactly right, Olivia. You are listening really well." If Olivia's hand does not go up, call on a peer sitting next to her to provide additional **repetition.** Then call on Olivia after the peer responds. Provide **specific academic and/or social praise** if her response is correct.

4. If Olivia does not respond correctly, consider whether or not the expectation is **developmentally appropriate.** For example, if the term *evaporate* is too complex, you can ask Olivia to tell you what happens when you boil water. Accept any response related to the concept and **positively reinforce.**

5. Use **shaping** to get Olivia closer to being able to define the word. For example, if she is able to say, "When water boils, it gets hot," then say, "Yes, and if it gets really hot, some of the water will start to disappear into the air. That's called evaporation." Use gestures

as you discuss this to **model** the concept and encourage Olivia to **imitate.** Then ask her, "Now can you tell me what evaporation means?" and **positively reinforce** if a correct response is given.

6. It may take several lessons to **shape** the student's behavior to be able to define the actual vocabulary word. In some instances, you may need to simply teach a concept as opposed to a specific word or alter the vocabulary word if it is too complex.

7. Repeat these procedures with five content area vocabulary words each week.

STUDENT: Darren

OBJECTIVE: Independently write name on all work completed in class

DATA COLLECTION PROCEDURES:

❑ Percentage Data

❑ Level of Independence Data

☑ Individualized Rating System

❑ Frequency Data

❑ Yes/No Data

EXPLANATION OF
DATA COLLECTION PROCEDURES:
0. Wrote 0 letters independently
1. Wrote 1 letter independently
2. Wrote 2–3 letters independently
3. Wrote 4–5 letters independently
4. Wrote entire name independently

TEACHING PROCEDURES:

1. Use **shaping procedures** to teach Darren to write his name independently. Begin by writing his name on the top of the paper, but leave out the last letter. Encourage Darren to complete his name by writing the last letter. Use **least-to-most prompts** if necessary. Provide **positive reinforcement** once Darren writes the letter independently or with prompting.

2. Once Darren consistently writes the last letter of his name, begin leaving out the last two letters. Encourage him to complete his name by writing the last two letters. Use **least-to-most prompts** if necessary. Provide **positive reinforcement** once he writes the letters independently or with prompting.

3. Continue to leave out one more letter each time Darren is consistently able to write the number of letters left out until mastery of writing his name is achieved.

4. Provide multiple opportunities for Darren to write part or all of his name each day by having him write his name on the top of all of his work.

STUDENT: Aaron

OBJECTIVE: Raise hand to correctly answer a question at least twice during whole-group instruction lessons across five consecutive school days

DATA COLLECTION PROCEDURES:

☐ Percentage Data

☐ Level of Independence Data

☐ Individualized Rating System

☐ Frequency Data

☑ Yes/No Data

> EXPLANATION OF
> DATA COLLECTION PROCEDURES:
>
> **Y** = Aaron raised his hand to correctly answer questions at least twice during each whole-group lesson and answered.
>
> **N** = Aaron needed prompting to raise his hand and answer questions during one or more whole-group instructional lessons.

TEACHING PROCEDURES:

1. During whole-group instruction, ask a question that is developmentally appropriate for Aaron (a question you are confident he can answer correctly).

2. If Aaron does not raise his hand, use **time delay** (pause and look at him with an expectant look/body language).

3. If Aaron still does not raise his hand, say his name, ask the question again and use **time delay** to encourage him to raise his hand to respond.

4. If Aaron still does not raise his hand, ask the question again in close proximity to him and physically prompt him to raise his hand (use **least-to-most prompts** for this physical guidance).

5. After Aaron raises his hand, call on him and provide **positive reinforcement** if he answers correctly.

6. If he doesn't answer correctly, use **least-to-most prompts** to provide the necessary supports for him to answer correctly (e.g., provide a fill-in, give a visual support, provide a choice). Provide **positive reinforcement** when he correctly responds with the given supports.

7. Repeat these procedures multiple times during whole-group lessons to allow for enough **repetition** until Aaron is raising his hand independently at least twice during each lesson.

Note: These teaching procedures should be used as often as possible with Aaron during whole-group instruction, still leaving many opportunities for other students to participate.

STUDENT: Blake

OBJECTIVE: Write one complete sentence using appropriate capitalization and ending punctuation about what is happening in a picture

DATA COLLECTION PROCEDURES:

☐ Percentage Data

☐ Level of Independence Data

☑ Individualized Rating System

☐ Frequency Data

☐ Yes/No Data

EXPLANATION OF
DATA COLLECTION PROCEDURES:

0. Did not write anything independently

1. Wrote one to two words independently

2. Wrote a short phrase independently

3. Wrote a complete sentence without appropriate capitalization and/or ending punctuation

4. Wrote a complete sentence using appropriate capitalization and ending punctuation

---

TEACHING PROCEDURES:

These teaching procedures can be used as part of a center activity. The center can be called "A Picture Is Worth a Thousand Words," and there can be a set of pictures to choose from and write about. Expectations for all students can be differentiated based on their present levels of performance. Blake will be expected to select a picture and write one complete sentence independently.

1. Allow Blake to choose a picture. If he does not choose a picture, hold up two choices and let him pick one (**prompt** if necessary).

2. Ask Blake to tell you what he sees in the picture. If he responds with a complete sentence, provide **positive reinforcement.** If he responds with only one or two words, a short phrase, or does not respond at all, use **least-to-most prompts** to enable him to respond with a complete sentence. For example, if there is a picture of a family at the beach, and Blake says, "beach," you can first prompt him by saying, "Tell me more." If he is unable to expand, point to something in the picture as a prompt. You can increase your prompts if necessary by asking questions about the picture.

3. After Blake responds with prompts, ask him to tell what he sees in the picture again. If he responds with a complete sentence, provide **positive reinforcement.** If he still is unable to respond with a complete sentence, use **modeling/request imitation** by providing the sentence and having him imitate.

4. You can also use **peer-mediated interventions** for Steps 1–3 by teaching Blake's peers how to assist him with stating a sentence about a picture.

5. Once Blake is able to select a picture and verbally provide a sentence about the picture independently, encourage him to write the sentence on paper. Use **most-to-least prompts** at first by writing the sentence he supplied and just leaving out the last word for him to complete. The next time, decrease the intensity of the prompt by writing half of the sentence and have him complete the rest. Continue to decrease the amount of words you provide until Blake is writing the sentence independently without any prompts at all.

Note: These procedures can be used across curriculum areas (reading, science, math, social studies) to provide many learning opportunities.

Behavior Teaching Plans

STUDENT: Leonard

OBJECTIVE: Protest appropriately by using a calm voice and positive language independently

DATA COLLECTION PROCEDURES:

☐ Percentage Data
☑ Level of Independence Data
☐ Individualized Rating System
☐ Frequency Data
☐ Yes/No Data

EXPLANATION OF
DATA COLLECTION PROCEDURES:

1. Maximum Prompting:
Needed teacher support to be redirected back to task

2. Moderate Prompting:
Needed the teacher to model an appropriate protest to imitate

3. Minimal Prompting:
Needed a verbal prompt or visual cue

4. Independent:
No assistance needed

TEACHING PROCEDURES:

1. When Leonard engages in negative behaviors when protesting, such as using a loud voice, offensive language, aggression, crying, or whining, intervene by using **modeling/request imitation** to correct the behavior. For example, if he screams out, "I don't want to do this stupid math!" when presented with an assignment, in a calm voice, model, "I might need a little help with this," and encourage him to imitate.

2. Once Leonard imitates, provide **positive reinforcement** by giving specific social praise and then say something such as, "Now let's try that again." Present the assignment again to provide an opportunity for him to protest appropriately without having to rely on imitating your model. If Leonard protests appropriately,

provide **positive reinforcement** and assist him as requested until he is able to continue without protest.

3. If Leonard does not protest appropriately, use **modeling/request imitation** again or **prompting/fading** procedures to encourage a positive response. Examples of prompts may include gestures such as putting a finger to your lips to indicate using a quiet voice, visual prompts such as **cue cards,** or verbal prompts such as "Use a calm voice please." Be sure to fade out prompts until Leonard is able to perform independently.

Note: It is important not to positively reinforce escape-motivated behavior. In other words, you should not allow Leonard to escape from required tasks simply because he protested appropriately. Instead, teach him protests that enable him to receive necessary supports. For example, you can teach him to request to work with a peer, to use alternate learning materials, to work independently in a quiet area, to work while listening to music, or any other support that can enable him to comply with the demands in a positive manner. If there are no supports that would enable Leonard to do so, consider if the request is developmentally appropriate.

STUDENT: Jeffrey

OBJECTIVE: Put class work away to finish at a later time without disruption every time requested to do so

DATA COLLECTION PROCEDURES:

❑ Percentage Data

❑ Level of Independence Data

❑ Individualized Rating System

❑ Frequency Data

☑ Yes/No Data

> EXPLANATION OF
> DATA COLLECTION PROCEDURES:
>
> **Y** = Jeffrey put his work away to finish later without disruption each time during the day
>
> **N** = Jeffrey needed teacher assistance to put his work away or did so with disruption at least once during the day

TEACHING PROCEDURES:

1. Create a folder that says something such as "To Finish Later." Use **direct instruction** teaching procedures to teach Jeffrey how to use the folder. Provide a rationale for why it is important to finish work later without disruption. Present the expectations by telling Jeffrey that when the class needs to move on to another activity or leave the classroom, he will put unfinished work in the folder. Reassure him that there will be an opportunity to finish the work that gets put in the folder. Demonstrate how to use the folder. Provide guided practice to allow Jeffrey to demonstrate the proper use of the folder. Conduct independent practice using the procedures in Steps 2–3.

2. **Shape** Jeffrey's ability to put work away for later by allowing him to get back to the folder and finish the work in a very short period of time (approximately 1 minute or so) the first time he uses the folder. The next time, make the wait time a little longer. Gradually add more and more time between the request to put the work in the folder and the opportunity to finish the work until Jeffrey is able to move on to another activity without stressing over unfinished work.

3. Provide **positive reinforcement** each time Jeffrey puts work in the folder without disruption. It may be helpful to create a **self-monitoring** tool in which he indicates whether or not work was put in the folder without disruption to increase independence and motivation.

STUDENT: Michael

OBJECTIVE: Respond appropriately when other students break a rule by ignoring the occurrence or writing a note to the teacher independently

DATA COLLECTION PROCEDURES:

☐ Percentage Data

☐ Level of Independence Data

☑ Individualized Rating System

☐ Frequency Data

☐ Yes/No Data

> EXPLANATION OF
> DATA COLLECTION PROCEDURES:
>
> **1. Maximum Prompting:**
> Could not ignore or write and needed teacher support to be redirected back to task
>
> **2. Moderate Prompting:**
> Needed teacher support to write a note
>
> **3. Minimal Prompting:**
> Needed a verbal prompt or visual cue
>
> **4. Independent:**
> No assistance needed

TEACHING PROCEDURES:

1. Provide **explicit instruction** to teach Michael how to respond when other students break a rule. This can be done using one-to-one instruction, small-group instruction, or whole-group instruction. Provide a rationale for why it is important to respond appropriately when others break rules. Demonstrate what should be done when others break rules. Involve Michael in guided practice activities through role-play opportunities. Continue guided practice activities until he responds appropriately at least 80% of the time during those activities. During independent practice, use the procedures that follow.

2. Provide a **self-monitoring** tool for Michael to use to record the number of times he responds appropriately when other students break a rule. Be sure to include the options for how to respond appropriately (ignoring or writing a note to the teacher) on the actual tool being used.

3. When you observe Michael using the self-monitoring tool, provide **positive reinforcement** by giving specific social praise. If he engages in inappropriate responses to rule breaking, such as yelling out to report the occurrence or directly challenging the peer who broke the rule, use **prompting/fading** procedures to positively redirect him. For example, provide a gestural prompt by

pointing to the self-monitoring tool or a verbal prompt such as, "Remember, you can choose to ignore or write a note." Be sure to fade the prompts being used to ensure Michael learns to respond independently.

4. Teach Michael to generalize appropriate responding to rule breaking by using the self-monitoring tool across a variety of settings. Once the skill is generalized, begin to fade out the use of the self-monitoring tool.

STUDENT: Darrien

OBJECTIVE: Walk in line quietly keeping hands and feet away from others independently

DATA COLLECTION PROCEDURES:

❐ Percentage Data

❐ Level of Independence Data

☑ Individualized Rating System

❐ Frequency Data

❐ Yes/No Data

EXPLANATION OF
DATA COLLECTION PROCEDURES:

1. Maximum Prompting:
Needed physical assistance to stay in line

2. Moderate Prompting:
Walked in line, but needed prompting to keep hands and feet away from others

3. Minimal Prompting:
Needed prompting to walk quietly, but kept hands and feet away from others

4. Independent:
Walked appropriately with no prompting

TEACHING PROCEDURES:

1. Use the **shaping** procedure by first determining what Darrien is currently able to do when walking in line and then raising the expectation and positively reinforcing him for meeting that expectation to bring him closer to the objective. For example, if Darrien can already line up independently, the next step would be to teach him to remain in line.

2. Use **prompting/fading** procedures to teach Darrien to remain in line. For example, if he gets out of line, positively redirect (prompt) him to get back in line. You can do this with a gesture such as pointing to the line, a verbal prompt such as, "Get back in line, please," or with physical guidance, such as gently guiding him back into line. Be sure to fade the prompts being used by decreasing the intensity of your prompts each time. If Darrien requires constant prompting, you may need to provide **most-to-least prompts** and then gradually fade out the level of your prompts. For example, at first you may need to walk right next to him while he is walking in the line or hold his hand while walking in line and then gradually fade out your assistance.

3. Provide **positive reinforcement** when Darrien meets the expectations.

4. As he meets the expectations set, raise the expectation so that it is closer to the desired objective. For example, once Darrien can walk in line independently until reaching the destination, then the expectation can include keeping his hands and feet away from others independently. Keep raising the expectation using **shaping** and **prompting/fading** procedures until the desired objective is met.

STUDENT: Samantha (a student with autism who is nonverbal)

OBJECTIVE: Stay in line when going through the cafeteria line and remain quiet or speak at a soft volume

DATA COLLECTION PROCEDURES:

❒ Percentage Data

❒ Level of Independence Data

❒ Individualized Rating System

❒ Frequency Data

☑ Yes/No Data

EXPLANATION OF
DATA COLLECTION PROCEDURES:

Y = Samantha stayed in line and was quiet until she received her lunch without teacher supports.

N = Samantha did not stay in line and/or was not quiet until she received her lunch, or she required prompting.

TEACHING PROCEDURES:

1. Develop a **Social Story** that explains the procedures for going through the lunch line (include the expectations of staying in line and remaining quiet) using PowerPoint. Use picture symbols throughout the story to enhance comprehension. Insert pictures of Samantha meeting the expectations. If possible, use **video self-modeling** by taking video clips of Samantha meeting the expectations and inserting those video clips into the Social Story for Samantha to watch. You can also use **video modeling** by inserting video clips of other students meeting the expectations.

2. While reading the story to Samantha, ask her questions that allow her to respond by pointing to the correct responses, such as "Where do you stand when you go to the cafeteria?" (Samantha points to the line). If Samantha does not respond or responds incorrectly when you ask her questions about the story, use **prompting/ fading procedures** to ensure successful responding. Provide **positive reinforcement** after she responds correctly.

3. **Shape** Samantha's ability to wait in line appropriately by only having her wait behind one or two students at first. Once she waits appropriately with only one or two students in front of her, provide **positive reinforcement** and increase the number of students in front of her the next time to three or four students. Continue this pattern until she can wait appropriately even if she has to wait for a whole class to go before her.

4. If Samantha still has difficulty waiting in line and remaining quiet, you can use **visual cues** by showing her pictures that represent standing in line and being quiet.

5. It may also be helpful to use a **self-monitoring tool** that allows Samantha to indicate whether she waited in line appropriately or not. The self-monitoring tool can have the visual cues right on it.

STUDENT: Paul

OBJECTIVE: Go to a "safe place" when extremely frustrated for 5 minutes and then return to the appropriate activity

DATA COLLECTION PROCEDURES:

❐ Percentage Data

❐ Level of Independence Data

❐ Individualized Rating System

❐ Frequency Data

☑ Yes/No Data

> EXPLANATION OF
> DATA COLLECTION PROCEDURES:
>
> **Y** = If Paul got extremely frustrated, he went to a safe place for 5 minutes and then returned to work area without prompting.
>
> **N** = Paul needed prompting to go to the safe place.
>
> **Note:** If Paul does not get extremely frustrated, do not take data on that day.

TEACHING PROCEDURES:

1. Teach Paul how to recognize his emotions by creating visual representations of different emotions leading up to "extremely frustrated," and list what things usually make him feel each emotion (happy, a little upset or anxious, frustrated, extremely frustrated). For example, for happy you can use a picture of a smiling child (or a picture of Paul smiling) and then have Paul tell you times that he is happy. List the examples of times when he is happy next to the picture. Do this for all of the emotions you choose to teach Paul, including "extremely frustrated." *The Incredible 5-Point Scale* is a good resource for this step (Buron & Curtis, 2003). Sometimes it is helpful to pair emotions with numbers, colors, objects, or symbols.

2. Use **direct instruction** teaching procedures to teach Paul options for what to do when he is a little upset, when he is frustrated, and when he is extremely frustrated. This can be done as a whole-group or small-group lesson. Designate a "safe place" in the room where Paul can go to when extremely frustrated to calm down. He can have access to some calming objects or activities for the 5 minutes that he is there. Teach Paul to set a timer for 5 minutes when he gets to the safe place.

3. After the direct instruction lesson has been provided and Paul was able to demonstrate how to go to the safe place during guided and independent practice, provide **positive reinforcement** when he goes to the safe place independently if he gets extremely frustrated at any time throughout the school day.

4. If Paul does not go to the safe place when extremely frustrated, use **prompting/fading procedures** to help him to do so. Provide **positive reinforcement** when he does indeed go.

Note: Some may consider the safe place as an opportunity for Paul to escape from demands. In a way it is, but students with ASD in general education classrooms have quite a lot to deal with on a regular basis. This may cause emotional dysregulation some of the time. Therefore, having a safe place for him to go is actually a proactive coping strategy that he can learn to prevent aggressive and disruptive behaviors. Because he is only there for 5 minutes and then goes back to the task at hand, he is not permanently escaping the demands. The idea is that he will be better able to deal with the demands if he is in a calm state, which will allow him to ask for the assistance he may need or use the communication or social interaction skills required to make it through the challenge.

Social Interaction Teaching Plans

STUDENT: Rodney

OBJECTIVE: Engage in reciprocal play interactions with peers and adults for at least 5 minutes at a time

DATA COLLECTION PROCEDURES:

☐ Percentage Data
☑ Level of Independence Data
☐ Individualized Rating System
☐ Frequency Data
☐ Yes/No Data

> EXPLANATION OF
> DATA COLLECTION PROCEDURES:
>
> **1. Maximum Prompting:**
> Needed continuous prompts to engage
>
> **2. Moderate Prompting:**
> Needed prompts throughout the 5 minutes, but not continuously
>
> **3. Minimal Prompting:**
> Needed 2–3 prompts during the 5 minutes
>
> **4. Independent:**
> Engaged for 5 minutes with no prompts

TEACHING PROCEDURES:

1. Begin the activity by **following** Rodney's **lead** (playing with what he is currently attending to) or initiating play with Rodney using materials he is not currently playing with.

2. As you begin interacting with Rodney, make a comment, ask a question, or give a direction, and use **time delay** (pause with an expectant look/body language) to encourage him to respond.

3. If he doesn't respond, use **prompting/fading procedures** to provide the necessary supports for him to engage. Consider the following example: Rodney is playing with trains and you join him and say, "I want a train to play with, too." If he doesn't respond, you can repeat the comment, use a gestural prompt such as putting

your hand out for a train, use a verbal prompt such as "Give me a train," or point to a train that you want. It is important, however, to fade out the prompts you are using so Rodney will learn to respond to comments, questions, and directions without the use of prompts.

4. Attempt to engage Rodney in as many back-and-forth exchanges as possible throughout the play routine. Think of this interaction as a rubber band that you are continually stretching to get it to be as long as possible without breaking.

5. Use **positive reinforcement** throughout this interaction when Rodney responds appropriately by giving smiles, high fives, specific positive praise, and allowing access to the materials Rodney wants during the play activity.

STUDENT: Felicia

OBJECTIVE: Greet at least one student when entering the classroom each morning

DATA COLLECTION PROCEDURES:

❐ Percentage Data

❐ Level of Independence Data

❐ Individualized Rating System

❐ Frequency Data

☑ Yes/No Data

> EXPLANATION OF
> DATA COLLECTION PROCEDURES:
> **Y** = Felicia independently greeted at least one peer
> **N** = Felicia needed prompting to greet a peer

TEACHING PROCEDURES:

1. Recruit a few peers in the classroom who are willing to provide **peer-mediated interventions** to teach Felicia how to greet other students.

2. Select one peer each morning to initiate a greeting with her. Encourage the peer to use whatever language is age-appropriate, such as "What's up, Felicia?" or "Hey, Felicia."

3. Instruct the peer to wait to initiate the greeting until the peer is in close proximity to Felicia. Encourage the peer to speak loud enough for Felicia to hear and to use **time delay** to encourage her to respond.

4. If Felicia responds, encourage the peer to **provide positive reinforcement** such as complimenting Felicia's outfit or making a positive conversational comment.

5. If Felicia doesn't respond, encourage the peer to repeat the greeting one or two more times. If still no response, use **prompting/fading procedures** to teach Felicia how to respond. This may include using visual prompts such as writing a greeting on a cue card that she can read, gestural prompts such as pointing to the peer that is greeting her, or verbal prompts such as saying, "Felicia, John said hello." Just be sure to fade out the intensity of your prompts to promote independence.

6. Once Felicia can respond to greetings from peers, teach the peers to use **time delay** to encourage Felicia to initiate the greeting. Use **cue cards** to **prompt** the student if necessary, but be sure to **fade out** the use of the cue cards to promote independence.

STUDENT: Jack

OBJECTIVE: Independently respond to peer initiations during recess in a positive manner (this may include making a positive comment to the peer, offering play materials to the peer, making eye contact and smiling at the peer, or asking the peer a question)

DATA COLLECTION PROCEDURES:

☐ Percentage Data

☑ Level of Independence Data

☐ Individualized Rating System

☐ Frequency Data

☐ Yes/No Data

EXPLANATION OF DATA COLLECTION PROCEDURES:
1. Maximum Prompting: Needed teacher prompting to respond
2. Moderate Prompting: Needed peers to prompt him to respond
3. Minimal Prompting: Needed peers to use time delay and/or repeat the initiation more than once
4. Independent: Responded to the majority of peer initiations without assistance

TEACHING PROCEDURES:

1. Encourage a peer to join Jack in whatever he is engaging with **(follow the student's lead).** For example, if Jack is playing with the steering wheel on the play structure, encourage the peer to join him at the steering wheel.

2. Encourage the peer to initiate an interaction by either making a comment or asking a question to Jack. For example, the peer may say, "Can I play, too?" "I want to drive, too." "Can I have a turn?" or "Where are you going in your car?" Or the peer can simply approach Jack, make eye contact, smile, say "hi," and wait for him to respond in a positive manner.

3. If Jack does not respond in a positive manner, provide facilitation as necessary. First, encourage the peer to make another initiation and then use **time delay.** If Jack still does not respond in a positive manner, join the play. For example, you can respond to the peer as you would have liked Jack to respond by saying something such as, "Climb in the car; we're driving to the beach!"

4. Continue to facilitate the play between the peer and Jack by **modeling** appropriate responses for Jack and encouraging him to **imitate.** If Jack attempts to move away from the peer, use **positive redirection** and **prompting/fading procedures** to encourage Jack to engage in a play interaction with the peer.

5. Be sure to provide **positive reinforcement** to the peer for all attempts to initiate positive interactions with the student.

STUDENT: Ethan

OBJECTIVE: Independently wait for a turn and take a turn during simple structured games/activities

DATA COLLECTION PROCEDURES:

❐ Percentage Data

☑ Level of Independence Data

❐ Individualized Rating System

❐ Frequency Data

❐ Yes/No Data

EXPLANATION OF
DATA COLLECTION PROCEDURES:

1. Maximum Prompting:
Needed physical prompts throughout

2. Moderate Prompting:
Needed verbal or gestural prompts to wait for a turn and take a turn

3. Minimal Prompting:
Able to take a turn, but needed prompts to wait and pay attention

4. Independent:
Waited and took turns without prompts

TEACHING PROCEDURES:

1. Start by setting up a highly structured game by choosing simple board games that have obvious starts and ends to each turn or using simple play activities. Examples of simple turn-taking activities include adding blocks to a tower, throwing bean bags into a box, or matching activities.

2. When first teaching this objective, play the game with Ethan and one other peer.

3. Start the turn-taking process by saying something such as, "My turn," and model what is expected. Then have the peer do the same.

4. If Ethan does not independently respond when it is his turn, use **least-to-most prompts.** You can prompt him by pushing a play object closer to him, giving him a play object, using a gestural prompt such as pointing to a play object, providing a verbal prompt such as "It's your turn, Ethan," or providing physical assistance if necessary. Be sure to fade out the prompts you are using until Ethan can respond independently.

5. Provide **positive reinforcement** after Ethan takes his turn.

6. If Ethan does not wait appropriately when you and the peer are taking a turn, use **least-to-most prompts** to keep him engaged. You can prompt him to pay attention by pointing, giving verbal

prompts, asking him questions, or giving him tasks to do between turns, such as giving the peer something.

7. Provide many **repetitions** of this turn-taking sequence to provide enough learning opportunities.

8. Once Ethan can wait and take turns with you and a peer, fade yourself out of the play until he can play with the peer without you. Once he can play independently with one peer, add another peer to the game.

STUDENT: Jackson

OBJECTIVE: Independently offer materials to a peer when a peer asks for something

DATA COLLECTION PROCEDURES:

☐ Percentage Data

☑ Level of Independence Data

☐ Individualized Rating System

☐ Frequency Data

☐ Yes/No Data

> EXPLANATION OF
> DATA COLLECTION PROCEDURES:
>
> **1. Maximum Prompting:**
> Needed physical prompts
>
> **2. Moderate Prompting:**
> Needed verbal or gestural prompts
>
> **3. Minimal Prompting:**
> Needed the peer to restate two or three times or needed to use time delay
>
> **4. Independent:**
> Offered the peer the item without prompting

TEACHING PROCEDURES:

Use **peer-mediated interventions** to teach the peer how to encourage Jackson to respond to requests to give materials independently. Use the following procedures:

1. The peer should approach Jackson and get in close proximity. The peer then asks Jackson for something that Jackson has in his work area.

2. If Jackson gives the peer the item, the peer should provide **positive reinforcement** such as saying, "Thanks so much, Jackson!" and smiling.

3. If Jackson does not give the peer the item, the peer should **use least-to-most prompts** to encourage Jackson to respond. First, the peer can just try to use **time delay** to give Jackson an opportunity to respond. If still no response, the peer can ask one or two more times. If still no response, the peer can ask again and put out his or her hand as a gestural prompt. At that point, if Jackson doesn't respond, you should provide more intense prompting to ensure a successful response. Do not allow the peer to provide physical prompts.

4. Once Jackson gives the peer the item, even with prompting, provide **positive reinforcement.**

5. These procedures should be used across the school day within many different activities and with a variety of different peers to promote generalization.

STUDENT: Whitney

OBJECTIVE: Offer a compliment to a peer at least once during the school day

DATA COLLECTION PROCEDURES:

☐ Percentage Data

☐ Level of Independence Data

☐ Individualized Rating System

☐ Frequency Data

☑ Yes/No Data

EXPLANATION OF
DATA COLLECTION PROCEDURES:

Y = Whitney complimented a peer at least once during the school day without teacher assistance or reminders.

N = Whitney did not compliment a peer at least once during the school day or needed teacher assistance to do so.

TEACHING PROCEDURES:

1. Develop a **Social Story** that teaches Whitney what compliments are, how to give compliments, when to give compliments, and how her peers usually feel when they receive compliments.

2. Provide a lesson either as a whole-group or small-group using **direct instruction** teaching procedures:

    Introduction: Discuss importance of giving compliments. Ask students to talk about how they feel when they receive a compliment and how they feel when they give a compliment.

    Lesson Presentation: The Social Story can be used as part of the lesson presentation. Ask comprehension questions about the story using **prompting/fading procedures** to help Whitney respond if necessary.

    Guided Practice: Engage students in role play to demonstrate how to give compliments.

    Independent Practice: Engage the students in an activity such as an art project or writing task and tell them they must share their work with at least one peer during the activity. The students will practice giving compliments when peers share their work. Provide feedback when students give or attempt to give compliments.

    Closure/Generalization: Review Social Story, and continually remind students throughout the day to give compliments when opportunities arise. Provide **positive reinforcement** when students are observed giving compliments to peers.

3. Share the Social Story with Whitney each day until she is giving at least one compliment to a peer each day without prompting to do so.

4. It may be helpful for Whitney to use a **self-monitoring** tool to indicate whether or not she offered a compliment each day.

D

Communication Teaching Plans

· ·

STUDENT: Jennifer

OBJECTIVE: Independently point to request desired items while making eye contact or naming the item

DATA COLLECTION PROCEDURES:

❏ Percentage Data

☑ Level of Independence Data

❏ Individualized Rating System

❏ Frequency Data

❏ Yes/No Data

> **EXPLANATION OF DATA COLLECTION PROCEDURES:**
>
> **1. Maximum Prompting:** Needed physical assistance
>
> **2. Moderate Prompting:** Needed modeling or verbal prompts
>
> **3. Minimal Prompting:** Needed time delay or withholding of items
>
> **4. Independent:** No assistance needed

TEACHING PROCEDURES:

1. Use **environmental arrangements** to provide opportunities for Jennifer to request items from others. For example, hold something out of reach, place something on a shelf that is out of reach, give small amounts so Jennifer will need to request more, or entice her by showing something that she would want to have.

2. When Jennifer indicates desire for the item by grabbing, whining, or reaching, use **time delay** to encourage her to point and make eye contact or name the item. If she doesn't respond, use **embedded discrete trials** to teach her to point. For example, first present an opportunity for Jennifer to point by showing something. If she doesn't point, use **modeling/request imitation** to encourage her to point. If no response, provide a gestural, verbal, or physical prompt.

Once Jennifer responds by pointing, provide **positive reinforcement** by giving her the item. Use **repetition** by presenting many **embedded discrete trials** across a variety of activities and settings until Jennifer is able to point independently.

3. Once she is able to point independently, **shape** the behavior by increasing the expectation to pointing and making eye contact or naming the item. Provide **positive reinforcement** only when Jennifer points and makes eye contact or names the item. Use **embedded discrete trials** to teach the new expectation.

STUDENT: Gavin

OBJECTIVE: Independently use simple sentences to make requests across a variety of classroom routines and activities

DATA COLLECTION PROCEDURES:

❐ Percentage Data

☑ Level of Independence Data

❐ Individualized Rating System

❐ Frequency Data

❐ Yes/No Data

> EXPLANATION OF
> DATA COLLECTION PROCEDURES:
>
> **1. Maximum Prompting:**
> Needed the entire sentence modeled
>
> **2. Moderate Prompting:**
> Needed part of the sentence modeled after using 1–2 words or a short phrase
>
> **3. Minimal Prompting:**
> Needed a verbal reminder to ask with a complete sentence, but did not need the actual sentence modeled
>
> **4. Independent:**
> Always used complete sentences to make requests

TEACHING PROCEDURES:

1. Use **environmental arrangements** to create opportunities for Gavin to make requests. For example, do not provide all of the materials he needs to complete an activity to provide an opportunity for him to request the necessary materials. If Gavin requests using simple sentences, provide **positive reinforcement** by giving him what was requested.

2. If Gavin requests using one- or two-word utterances or a short phrase, use **prompting/fading procedures** to encourage him to use a simple sentence. For example, if he says, "Scissors," get the scissors, show him you have the scissors, but do not give them to him right away. Use **time delay** to see if he will then request the scissors using a simple sentence. If not, say something such as, "If you want the scissors, ask for them." If still no response say, "Say, 'I need scissors, please,'" and have Gavin imitate. Be sure to fade out the amount of words you are providing with each request to increase Gavin's independence.

3. It is important to teach Gavin a variety of simple sentences that can be used to request items, such as, "I want scissors," "I need scissors, please," "Can I have scissors?"and so forth. If you only teach one specific sentence, he may be more robotic than natural when making requests. Also use natural inflection when modeling to prevent him from sounding robotic.

STUDENT: Christopher

OBJECTIVE: Respond to comments related to current activity independently

DATA COLLECTION PROCEDURES:

❐ Percentage Data

☑ Level of Independence Data

❐ Individualized Rating System

❐ Frequency Data

❐ Yes/No Data

> EXPLANATION OF
> DATA COLLECTION PROCEDURES:
>
> **1. Maximum Prompting:**
> Responds by imitating the response
>
> **2. Moderate Prompting:**
> Responds given a fill-in or a choice
>
> **3. Minimal Prompting:**
> Responds given time delay, if the comment is repeated, or if the comment is restated
>
> **4. Independent:**
> Responds to the majority of comments

TEACHING PROCEDURES:

1. When Christopher is engaged in an activity, make a comment about what he is doing.

2. If he responds, provide **positive reinforcement** by making an additional positive comment or specific praise, smiling, or joining him in the activity if that would be enjoyable to him.

3. If Christopher doesn't respond to the comment, use **time delay** to encourage him to respond. For example, while drawing you might say, "I like your picture." If he responds, provide positive reinforcement. For example, if Christopher then says, "I'm drawing a sun," you might smile and say, "Your sun looks beautiful!"

4. If Christopher doesn't respond given the time delay, try stating the comment again or rephrasing the comment in a way you think he may respond. If still no response, use **embedded discrete trials** to ensure a response. For example, state the comment again, and if Christopher doesn't respond, provide a prompt. The prompt may include a fill-in so he can respond to the comment. For example, you may say, "I'm drawing a _____," to encourage Christopher to fill in the sentence to respond to the comment "I like your picture." You can also use a gestural prompt, such as pointing to the picture of the sun after making the comment to encourage him to respond. Once Christopher responds, provide **positive reinforcement.** Be sure to fade out the types of prompts you provide as

you provide additional **embedded discrete trials** for more learning opportunities. Although you can ask Christopher a question as a prompt, such as "What are you drawing?" try to avoid that if possible, because then he is answering a question not responding to a comment.

5. Use **peer-mediated interventions** to teach peers to use these procedures to encourage Christopher to respond to comments from peers.

6. Provide multiple opportunities throughout the day across a variety of activities and settings to promote **generalization.**

STUDENT: Jordan

OBJECTIVE: Independently respond to indicate whether he wants something or not using "yes" and "no" cards

DATA COLLECTION PROCEDURES:

❐ Percentage Data

❐ Level of Independence Data

☑ Individualized Rating System

❐ Frequency Data

❐ Yes/No Data

> EXPLANATION OF
> DATA COLLECTION PROCEDURES:
>
> **1. Maximum Prompting:**
> Responds with physical assistance
>
> **2. Moderate Prompting:**
> Responds when given a prompt such as pushing the card forward, pointing to the card, or tapping on the card
>
> **3. Minimal Prompting:**
> Responds when both cards are pushed closer to him
>
> **4. Independent:**
> Gives the yes and no cards without assistance

TEACHING PROCEDURES:

1. Use **environmental arrangements** by placing desired items out of reach or giving only small portions of the desired items to allow opportunities for Jordan to communicate. When teaching "yes," be sure to use items you know Jordan wants. When teaching "no," be sure to use items you know Jordan does not want at that time.

2. Use **embedded discrete trials** to teach Jordan to answer a question to indicate whether he wants something or not. For example, at snack time give Jordan his napkin and place a cookie in your hand, but out of Jordan's reach. Then ask, "Do you want a cookie?" First use **time delay** (pause with an expectant look/body language) to see if Jordan will show/hand you his yes/no card. If he doesn't respond or grabs for the cookie, use **least-to-most prompting** to get him to show or give you the card. Prompts can include moving both cards closer to Jordan to encourage him to pick one, moving only the yes card closer to Jordan's hand, pointing to the yes card, tapping the yes card, placing Jordan's hand on the card, helping Jordan to pick up the card and give it to you. Once Jordan gives you the card, provide **positive reinforcement** by providing social praise and giving him a piece of the cookie.

3. Use the same teaching procedures listed above to teach Jordan to use the "yes" and "no" cards for preferred and nonpreferred items across a variety of different routines and activities in the classroom.

STUDENT: Katherine

OBJECTIVE: Answer simple questions related to recent activities with 80% accuracy

DATA COLLECTION PROCEDURES:

☑ Percentage Data

❏ Level of Independence Data

❏ Individualized Rating System

❏ Frequency Data

❏ Yes/No Data

> EXPLANATION OF
> DATA COLLECTION PROCEDURES:
> Each time you ask Katherine a question, indicate **correct** if she answers without any prompts and **incorrect** if she requires prompts or does not answer. Divide the number of correct responses by the total number of questions asked to get a percentage correct.

TEACHING PROCEDURES:

1. Immediately after an activity such as an academic lesson, recess, lunch, music, physical education, or art, ask Katherine a simple question pertaining to the activity. Some examples of questions include: "What song did you sing in music?" "What did you eat for lunch?" "What game did you play in physical education?"

2. If Katherine responds accurately, provide **positive reinforcement.** If her answer is only a one-word response or a short phrase, still accept the response and positively reinforce. The goal here is to get her to process a question and respond appropriately, even if the answer is not in a complete sentence.

3. If Katherine does not respond, repeats the question, or gives an incorrect response, repeat the question one more time and use **time delay.**

4. If still no response, repeat the question using **prompting/fading** procedures to enable her to respond successfully. Use the following **least-to-most prompt** sequence:
   a. Restate the question another way.
   b. Use a fill-in. "In music, we sang _____." If you do use a fill-in, after Katherine fills in, restate the question again so she has an opportunity to respond without the prompt of a fill-in.
   c. Provide a choice. "Did you eat chicken nuggets or a hot dog?" If you provide a choice, make sure you don't always put the correct answer last to be sure Katherine is not just repeating the last word you said.

    d. Use **visual cues** when providing a choice.

    e. Use **modeling/request imitation** by supplying the answer and having Katherine imitate the response. After she imitates, restate the question again so she has an opportunity to respond without the model.

5. Provide **positive reinforcement** after she responds (even if prompting was needed).

STUDENT: Jahmal

OBJECTIVE: Use an augmentative communication device to respond to questions during instructional lessons

DATA COLLECTION PROCEDURES:

☑ Percentage Data

❏ Level of Independence Data

❏ Individualized Rating System

❏ Frequency Data

❏ Yes/No Data

> EXPLANATION OF
> DATA COLLECTION PROCEDURES:
> Each time you ask Jahmal a question, indicate **correct** if he answers correctly using the communication device without any prompts. Indicate **incorrect** if he requires prompts or does not answer. Divide the number of correct responses by the total number of questions asked to get a percentage correct.

TEACHING PROCEDURES:

An augmentative and alternative communication (AAC) assessment should be conducted to determine the most appropriate device for Jahmal based on his needs and present levels of performance. Once a device is selected, provide instruction on the use of the device and a great deal of practice using it. Once he is using the device easily, use the teaching procedures below.

1. Preload the device with pictures related to the lesson you are teaching. The lesson can be related to reading, science, math, social studies, or any other subject.

2. Throughout the lesson ask questions to the class that Jahmal can respond to by selecting the appropriate picture on his AAC device.

3. If Jahmal raises his hand, call on him when appropriate and allow him an opportunity to respond. Provide sufficient **time delay** for processing and responding. If he responds accurately, provide **positive reinforcement.**

4. If Jahmal does not raise his hand, call on him as often as possible throughout the lesson to increase his learning opportunities and active engagement.

5. If Jahmal does not respond or responds incorrectly, use the following **least-to-most prompts** as needed:
   a. Restate the question.
   b. Point to a picture in the learning materials as a visual cue.
   c. Point to the device to encourage Jahmal to respond.

    d. Provide a fill-in ("Matter can be in the form of a liquid, solid, or a _____.").

    e. Provide a choice of two ("Did the boy win a bicycle or a computer?").

    f. Point to the correct answer on the device.

    g. Use **modeling/request imitation.**

    h. Provide physical prompts.

6. If any of the above prompts are used, restate the question again if possible to allow Jahmal an opportunity to respond without any prompts.

7. Provide **positive reinforcement** when Jahmal responds correctly, even if prompts were provided.

Independent Functioning Teaching Plans

. . . .

STUDENT: Brandon

OBJECTIVE: Transition from class to class independently for all six periods

DATA COLLECTION PROCEDURES:

❐ Percentage Data

❐ Level of Independence Data

❐ Individualized Rating System

☑ Frequency Data

❐ Yes/No Data

> EXPLANATION OF
> DATA COLLECTION PROCEDURES:
> Record the number of classes that Brandon walks to independently each day.

TEACHING PROCEDURES:

1. Develop a **self-monitoring tool** to assist Brandon in making the transition from class to class. The tool can include a schedule of the day with columns to check off when he gets to class. If bringing the necessary materials is a problem, a column can be added for materials so he can check for specific materials before walking to the appropriate class.

2. Use **peer-mediated interventions** to teach a peer to provide assistance to Brandon during transitions that would be gradually faded out. For example, the peer may initially walk Brandon to class each class period. Then gradually fade out the number of classes that the peer walks him to class. The peer can do that by asking Brandon what class is next and if he knows how to get there. If Brandon indicates the correct class and that he can get

there, the peer may just follow him without walking right next to him. Once Brandon can get to a class for several school days in a row with the peer following further and further behind, he can begin walking to that class without the peer.

3. Continue the procedures in Step 2 until the student is able to walk to all classes independently.

4. When the student is able to use the self-monitoring tool without peer support consistently, begin to **fade out** the use of the self-monitoring tool.

STUDENT: Nicholas

OBJECTIVE: Remain on task during independent work periods for 5 minutes

DATA COLLECTION PROCEDURES:

❐ Percentage Data

☑ Level of Independence Data

❐ Individualized Rating System

❐ Frequency Data

❐ Yes/No Data

EXPLANATION OF
DATA COLLECTION PROCEDURES:

1. Maximum Prompting:
Needed continual prompts to stay on task

2. Moderate Prompting:
Needed several prompts to stay on task

3. Minimal Prompting:
Needed 1–3 prompts to stay on task

4. Independent:
No assistance needed to stay on task for 5 minutes

TEACHING PROCEDURES:

1. Provide Nicholas with a task that is developmentally appropriate. This means a task he has the skills necessary to complete.

2. Demonstrate what Nicholas is supposed to do with the materials if it is a new task.

3. Give Nicholas a direction such as, "Now, you do it."

4. Provide **least-to-most prompts** throughout the activity to promote independent completion. For example, if Nicholas gets off task, you can prompt him with gestures such as pointing to his work, visual cues, verbal prompts, or assistance with the task.

5. Provide **positive reinforcement** for completing the whole task. If Nicholas needs more than positive reinforcement at the completion of the activity in order to remain on task, provide additional positive reinforcement throughout the activity. However, be sure to **fade out** the amount of positive reinforcement needed during task completion, because that takes away from his ability to attend and focus if he is continually seeking reinforcement each step along the way.

STUDENT: Kayla

OBJECTIVE: Choose from list of approved activities when finished with an assignment

DATA COLLECTION PROCEDURES:

☐ Percentage Data

☑ Level of Independence Data

☐ Individualized Rating System

☐ Frequency Data

☐ Yes/No Data

EXPLANATION OF
DATA COLLECTION PROCEDURES:

1. Maximum Prompting:
Needed physical assistance

2. Moderate Prompting:
Needed verbal prompts

3. Minimal Prompting:
Needed a gestural prompt

4. Independent:
No assistance needed to choose and begin an activity

TEACHING PROCEDURES:

1. Create a list of approved activities that students can choose from when they finish an assignment before the other students. This may include activities such as reading a book, drawing a picture, or writing a story.

2. Use **direct instruction** teaching procedures to teach the students what to do when they finish an assignment early. Provide a rationale for why it is important for students to remain engaged after they finish an assignment. Present how students would go about choosing an activity by pretending you are a student who finished early. Engage the students in guided practice by having them pretend they are finished with an assignment so they must choose an activity. Provide independent practice for Kayla by using the steps that follow.

3. Before she begins an assignment, review with her the options for what she can do when she is finished. If she chooses an activity independently when she finishes, provide **positive reinforcement.**

4. If Kayla does not choose an activity when she finishes, use **prompting/ fading** procedures to encourage her to do so. You can prompt her by pointing to a visual cue of the choices, giving her a verbal prompt, or physically assisting her to get her started on one of the activities. Just be sure to fade out any prompts you use. Provide **positive reinforcement** once she chooses and begins an activity.

STUDENT: Benjamin

OBJECTIVE: Makes transition from one activity to the next within the classroom independently

DATA COLLECTION PROCEDURES:

☐ Percentage Data

☑ Level of Independence Data

☐ Individualized Rating System

☐ Frequency Data

☐ Yes/No Data

> EXPLANATION OF
> DATA COLLECTION PROCEDURES:
>
> **1. Maximum Prompting:**
> Needed physical assistance
>
> **2. Moderate Prompting:**
> Needed many verbal prompts
>
> **3. Minimal Prompting:**
> Needed one or two verbal, visual, or gestural prompts each time
>
> **4. Independent:**
> No assistance needed to make transitions throughout the day

TEACHING PROCEDURES:

1. Create a **visual schedule** of the classroom routine. The schedule can consist of objects, pictures, symbols, or words, depending on what is developmentally appropriate for Benjamin.

2. Use the visual schedule to assist with transitioning by having Benjamin move the picture, symbol, or word for each activity to a column that says something such as "finished" at the conclusion of each activity.

3. After he moves the item over, ask him what comes next. If he answers independently, provide **positive reinforcement.** If he does not answer, use **least-to-most prompts** to encourage him to respond. You can prompt Benjamin by pointing to the picture, symbol, or word. You can also have him imitate after you give him a verbal prompt or use physical assistance to have him point to what comes next. Be sure to fade out any prompts you use.

4. If Benjamin then makes the transition appropriately, provide **positive reinforcement.** If he engages in negative behaviors and does not make the transition appropriately, use **least-to-most prompts** to help him transition. This can include gestural prompts such as pointing to where he needs to go, visual prompts such as showing the schedule or something that symbolizes where he needs to go, verbal prompts, or physical assistance if necessary. Be sure to **fade out** any prompts you use.

Note: It is recommended that you use flexible scheduling to assist Benjamin with transitions. Vary the types of activities (whole-group instruction, small-group instruction, independent work, cooperative work) so there are not two whole-group lessons one after the other or two small-group lessons, etc. Also, schedule highly preferred activities after nonpreferred activities to increase motivation.

STUDENT: Lauren

OBJECTIVE: Use the bathroom without adult support

DATA COLLECTION PROCEDURES:

☑ Percentage Data

☐ Level of Independence Data

☐ Individualized Rating System

☐ Frequency Data

☐ Yes/No Data

> EXPLANATION OF
> DATA COLLECTION PROCEDURES:
> Use a task analysis to indicate how many of the steps Lauren completed independently and how many she needed assistance with. Divide the number of steps she completed independently by the total number of steps to get a percentage correct.

TEACHING PROCEDURES:

1. Develop a **task analysis** for the steps of using the bathroom.

2. Create a **self-monitoring tool** that includes the steps in number order (and pictures of the steps if necessary).

3. Use **whole-task presentation chaining** to increase Lauren's independence using the self-monitoring tool when she uses the bathroom. **Prompting/fading procedures** should be used to add more independent steps each time she uses the bathroom.

4. Initially, provide **positive reinforcement** after each step even if done with support, but gradually **fade out** the positive reinforcement by eventually only reinforcing her independent steps. Once Lauren can complete all steps independently, only reinforce after all steps are completed.

Note: This objective requires that at least two adults be assigned to the classroom to allow one person to monitor Lauren during the bathroom routine and one person to remain with the rest of the students.

F

Blank Forms for Assessment, Goal Setting, and Data Collection

• •

Assessing Strengths and Interests: Student Interview
Assessing Strengths and Interests: Parent/Teacher Interview
Preference Assessment Recording Form
Assessing Communication Skills
Assessing Social Interaction Skills
Assessing Social Skills
Assessing Academic Skills
Assessing Problem Behavior
Self-Monitoring Example for Completing Assignments
Percentage Correct Data Sheet
Level of Independence Data Sheet
Frequency Data Sheet
Yes/No Data Collection Sheet
ABA Teaching Plan Template

Assessing Strengths and Interests: Student Interview

Opening statement	Student response
Tell me about your strengths and interests.	

Additional probing questions	Student response
What types of things do you like?	
What are you good at?	
What makes you happy?	
What are your favorite toys?	
What do you like to do?	
Who do you like to spend time with?	

(continued)

Additional probing questions	Student response
What are your favorite times of the day?	
What can you do that many other kids cannot do?	
What are your favorite places?	
What are some things in your house or school that you would never want to give up?	

Assessing Strengths and Interests: Parent/Teacher Interview

Date	Student's name	Interviewer	Individual responding

Opening statement	Parent/teacher response
Tell me about the student's strengths and interests.	

Additional probing questions	Parent/teacher response
What makes the student happy?	
How does the student prefer to spend his or her time?	
What are the student's favorite toys or activities?	
In what areas does the student excel?	
What about the student makes you proud?	

(continued)

Additional probing questions	Parent/teacher response
Who does the student like to spend time with?	
What are the student's favorite times of the day?	
What keeps the student's attention?	
What are the student's favorite places?	
What would the student never want to give up?	

Preference Assessment Recording Form

Student's name		Individual conducting assessment	
Date/activity	Choice 1	Choice 2	Selection

Assessing Communication Skills

Student's name		
Question	**Information gathered from interviews**	**Information gathered from direct observation**
How does the student express wants and needs?		
How does the student express frustration or anger?		
What types of directions can the student follow? (Consider one-step, multistep, simple, complex, academic, behavioral, social.)		
What types of questions can the student answer/ask? (Consider questions about academic content, common knowledge, the past, recent or very recent past, ongoing activities, the future, personal information.)		

(continued)

Assessing Communication Skills   *(continued)*

Student's name		
Question	**Information gathered from interviews**	**Information gathered from direct observation**
What types of comments does the student respond to/initiate? (Consider comments made during academic activities and social activities.)		
To what level can the student engage in conversation with adults/peers? (Consider topics, length of back-and-forth exchanges, ability to initiate conversations, join conversations, end conversations, remain on topic.)		

Assessing Social Interaction Skills

Student's name		
Question	**Information gathered from interviews**	**Information gathered from direct observation**
What is the student's ability to respond to joint attention bids from others? (Consider whether the student allows others to join in on what the student is currently engaged with; consider whether the student responds to comments, directions, or questions made by others verbally and/or nonverbally.)		
What is the student's ability to maintain joint attention with others? (Consider duration of time, types of activities.)		
What is the student's ability to initiate joint attention with others? (Consider verbal and nonverbal initiations, types of activities that stimulate initiations.)		
To what extent can the student engage in reciprocal social interactions with peers/adults? (Consider length of back-and-forth verbal and/or nonverbal interactions; consider social and academic activities.)		

Assessing Social Skills

Student's name		
Skill	**Independent**	**Level of prompting needed**
Shares materials during joint tasks		
Shares materials during independent/parallel tasks		
Responds when others offer a turn		
Offers a turn to others		
Maintains attention while waiting for a turn		
Offers help to others		
Accepts help from others		
Empathizes with the feelings of others		
Uses appropriate voice volume		
Uses appropriate space with a social partner		
Responds to greetings		
Initiates greetings		
Uses appropriate eye contact when interacting with others		
Gives compliments to others		
Receives compliments positively		
Maintains personal hygiene		
Responds appropriately to facial expressions of others		
Responds appropriately to body language of others		
Appropriately responds when others are in the way		
Compromises during academic and social activities		

Assessing Academic Skills

Student's name		
Academic area	**Results from formal/ standardized assessments**	**Results from informal assessments**
Reading (Consider phonemic awareness, phonics, fluency, comprehension, and vocabulary.)		
Math (Consider number concepts, computations, application, and problem solving.)		
Language arts (Consider listening, speaking, and writing.)		
Content area (Consider how students learn new concepts and vocabulary, participation in whole-group and small-group instruction, cooperative learning activities, and independent work.)		

Assessing Problem Behavior

Name of student	Description of problem behavior		
Name of assessor			
Hypothesis	Data collected through interview	Data collected through direct observation	Data collected through functional analysis
To communicate wants and needs			
To communicate frustration or anxiety due to skill deficit			
To gain social attention/ interaction			
To gain engagement or avoid disengagement/ boredom			

Self-Monitoring Example for Completing Assignments

Date	Student's name		
Name of assignment	**I finished the assignment (yes or no)**	**I turned in the assignment (yes or no)**	**Points earned (5 points for each assignment turned in)**
			Total points earned:

Percentage Correct Data Sheet. (*Key:* C, Correct; I, Incorrect.)

Student's name			Objective		
Trials	Date	Date	Date	Date	Date
10	C/I 100%	C/I 100%	C/I 100%	C/I 100%	C/I 100%
9	C/I 90%	C/I 90%	C/I 90%	C/I 90%	C/I 90%
8	C/I 80%	C/I 80%	C/I 80%	C/I 80%	C/I 80%
7	C/I 70%	C/I 70%	C/I 70%	C/I 70%	C/I 70%
6	C/I 60%	C/I 60%	C/I 60%	C/I 60%	C/I 60%
5	C/I 50%	C/I 50%	C/I 50%	C/I 50%	C/I 50%
4	C/I 40%	C/I 40%	C/I 40%	C/I 40%	C/I 40%
3	C/I 30%	C/I 30%	C/I 30%	C/I 30%	C/I 30%
2	C/I 20%	C/I 20%	C/I 20%	C/I 20%	C/I 20%
1	C/I 10%	C/I 10%	C/I 10%	C/I 10%	C/I 10%

Level of Independence Data Sheet. (1 = Maximum Prompting; 2 = Moderate Prompting; 3 = Minimal Prompting; 4 = Independent.)

Student's name							
Objective	**Date**	**Date**	**Date**	**Date**	**Date**	**Date**	**Date**
	4	4	4	4	4	4	4
	3	3	3	3	3	3	3
	2	2	2	2	2	2	2
	1	1	1	1	1	1	1
	Date	**Date**	**Date**	**Date**	**Date**	**Date**	**Date**
	4	4	4	4	4	4	4
	3	3	3	3	3	3	3
	2	2	2	2	2	2	2
	1	1	1	1	1	1	1
	Date	**Date**	**Date**	**Date**	**Date**	**Date**	**Date**
	4	4	4	4	4	4	4
	3	3	3	3	3	3	3
	2	2	2	2	2	2	2
	1	1	1	1	1	1	1

Frequency Data Sheet

Student's name		Objective				
	Date	**Date**	**Date**	**Date**	**Date**	**Date**
Total frequency of behavior per	10	10	10	10	10	10
	9	9	9	9	9	9
_____	8	8	8	8	8	8
	7	7	7	7	7	7
	6	6	6	6	6	6
	5	5	5	5	5	5
	4	4	4	4	4	4
	3	3	3	3	3	3
	2	2	2	2	2	2
	1	1	1	1	1	1
	0	0	0	0	0	0

Yes/No Data Collection Sheet

Student's name									
Objective	Date	Date	Date	Date	Date	Date	Date	Date	Date
	Y N	Y N	Y N	Y N	Y N	Y N	Y N	Y N	Y N
	Y N	Y N	Y N	Y N	Y N	Y N	Y N	Y N	Y N
	Y N	Y N	Y N	Y N	Y N	Y N	Y N	Y N	Y N
	Y N	Y N	Y N	Y N	Y N	Y N	Y N	Y N	Y N
	Y N	Y N	Y N	Y N	Y N	Y N	Y N	Y N	Y N
	Y N	Y N	Y N	Y N	Y N	Y N	Y N	Y N	Y N

ABA Teaching Plan Template

Student	Objective

Data Collection Procedures

❐ Percentage Data

❐ Level of Independence Data

❐ Individualized Rating System

❐ Frequency Data

❐ Yes/No Data

Explanation of Data Collection Procedures:

Teaching Procedures

1.

2.

3.

4.

5.

6.

7.

8.

9.

10.

Index

Page numbers followed by *f* indicate figures; those followed by *t* indicate tables.